LIVING ON THE
DEVIL'S
DOORSTEP

LIVING ON THE DEVIL'S DOORSTEP
The McClung Family Story

Floyd McClung

WORD BOOKS
PUBLISHER
WACO, TEXAS

WORD, CANADA
RICHMOND, B.C.

LIVING ON THE DEVIL'S DOORSTEP

ISBN 0-8499-3043-X

Printed in the United States of America

DEDICATION

To two of my favourite people in the whole world:
Not only do I love them as my children, but
I like them as friends!
With great affection I dedicate this book to
Misha and Matthew.

Grateful Acknowledgments

Although it has my name on the front cover, this book is more than my story. It is equally that of my beloved wife Sally, our children Misha and Matthew, and all the dear friends who have been part of our lives.

I am particularly grateful for Paul Conn, who heard me speak many years ago, and believed in me enough to write *Just Off Chicken Street*, a book about our experiences in Afghanistan. That book really paved the way for this one.

It is wonderful when someone you work with closely also becomes a good friend. Andy Butcher not only helped write this book, he has also endeared himself to Sally and me. In fact, I haven't given up on the idea that someday he and Mandy will work with us in Amsterdam!

I also wish to express my thanks to Noël Halsey and Janet Hall of Word Publishers. They have been a great encouragement and help, and have helped make the rough places smooth. Thank you, Noël and Janet.

There are many wonderful stories of changed lives not included here. There are also many special co-workers whose contributions have not been singled out. They each know who they are, and I am grateful for all they have given.

This book isn't intended to be exhaustive. I just want to share with you some of the amazing things that happened to our family while living in some pretty dangerous circumstances and to encourage - perhaps challenge - you to trust Him as He protects and provides for you. In one way we are all "living on the Devil's doorstep."

CONTENTS

One

Mourning the Night

Thick pungent smoke from a dozen flaming torches drifted into the greying twilight as a sombre funeral procession snaked its way slowly through one of the narrow canalside avenues in Amsterdam. A line of mourners followed solemnly behind a large black coffin carried by six grim-faced men. One of the women, at the head of the procession just behind the coffin, carried a small bouquet of flowers. Some of the others were weeping silently as they walked along.

The funeral procession moved slowly onto one of the small arch-backed bridges spanning the canal where the pallbearers stopped and lowered their burden. The silent mourners grouped around the coffin and immediately a large crowd of onlookers gathered around.

Why was the funeral being held so late at night - and in the heart of Amsterdam's Red Light District? Where were they going? Why had they stopped on the bridge? Pimps, prostitutes, pushers, passers-by and groups of tourists waited and watched expectantly.

Queues of cars and pedestrians formed quickly on the narrow, cobble-stoned streets on either side of the bridge as traffic quickly ground to a halt. Attracted by the noise of car horns and the angry demands of busy taxi-drivers to "get out of the way!", several of the prostitutes occupying rooms high up in the four-storey town houses appeared at the windows of their cramped little bed-sit rooms to peer down.

With several hundred people now crowded in the middle of one of the district's main thoroughfares, totally disrupting the normal pattern of events, I stepped on top of the black coffin and, interrupting the clamour, began to speak to the crowd.

"Why are you staring at these girls?" I asked, pointing to the near-naked girls sitting in small, smudged neon-lit windows.

"Why are you treating them this way? It makes no difference what *they* are doing. Why are *you* here window shopping in the neighbourhood?"

I was upset with the tourists visiting the live sex shows, peep show booths, porno cinemas and sex shops. Why were they laughing and smiling - trying to have a good time at the expense of others?

Then I told them that the funeral they were witnessing was for them! It was for all who had allowed something of themselves to die in Amsterdam. The funeral was for all who had been crippled by drugs and sold their souls to prostitution or pornography. I told them that the tears they saw on the faces of some of the mourners were no act; that the young people near them had wept for them as they had sensed just a small measure of God's grief over what He witnessed.

Scanning the crowd, I saw a man standing at the rear. He looked much like all the other middle-aged strollers who had been drawn by what was going on, but as I talked my eyes kept coming back to his face. As I spoke, I sensed that God was showing me things about him. Almost without pausing, I looked over towards him and called out a question:

"Why, sir, are you here tonight? You've got a wife and three children at home, haven't you? Don't you know that you are betraying their trust, their love, their faith in you?"

As I looked at other parts of the crowd, I didn't see him turn and back away quickly, muttering as he strode swiftly away an ashamed, "How did he know?" to one of the "mourners" who happened to be standing nearby. But I did notice straight-away a tight-lipped and furious looking man who had pushed his way through the crowd to stand on the bridge directly below me.

When he started to pull at my jacket, I knew that he wanted to interrupt, to stop me from continuing with the words God wanted me to share from His heart. But with my six-foot-six frame topping a large coffin, I seemed to be safely beyond grabbing reach, so I ignored him and preached on, talking over the top of his head into the large crowd.

I told them how much God's heart was broken by what He saw on the streets of Amsterdam, and in countless hidden rooms - about the pain and disappointment that wracked Him as He looked into their hearts and saw the way they abused His gifts of love and life. And I told them that even now He loved them. Despite everything - each lustful look, all the hateful thoughts and deeds - He loved them so intensely that He had come to earth and allowed their hardness and hatred to nail Him to a tree. He had died to set them free, to heal the wounds and hurts, to give them new life, with new hopes and dreams. I told them how much God cared.

As I finished and stepped down, people in the crowd stood silently, a little stunned by what they had just heard and seen. And while some swung back to whatever had occupied them a short while before, others stayed on, hovering uncertainly. To them the mourners - my co-workers - turned with listening ears, gentle questions, and an eagerness to show a concern and respect for their fears and their spiritual need.

The bridge gradually cleared and one of the pallbearers

caught my arm and told me that the would-be heckler was the proprietor of a nearby sex club, who had been incensed by what had happened as it had driven some potential customers away from his doors. He had spoken angrily and aggressively to several other members of the team and then stalked off in a rage.

I picked my way through the groups of people still talking - earnest conversations here and there about Jesus and His love for the people of the Red Light area of Amsterdam - and went over to where the protestor now stood outside his premises. It was a particularly shabby, seamy-looking sex club. I introduced myself and told him that I was sorry he had been offended - but that I could not apologise for what I had said, or how it had affected his trade. I explained that we loved him and were concerned for him as a person. He just glared venomously back at me.

"Look, Floyd McClung, Mr. Preacher, whatever-your-name-is. If you ever set foot back here again, I will stick this in your back and you will be found floating face down in the canal. Do you understand me?" The blade in his hand and the matter-of-fact flatness with which he delivered the words, without a trace of melodrama, chilled my heart momentarily. Looking him in the eyes, I reminded him of our genuine interest in him as an individual, and slowly turned around to walk away.

As we parted, my heart pounding with fear, I wondered again fleetingly what it was that had brought me halfway round the world to hold a funeral for a city full of people where you could pay for virtually anything you wanted to buy, but you couldn't even start to give someone that which no amount of money can ever purchase.

Amsterdam is proudly proclaimed as "The Venice of the North" to its countless sight-seeing visitors. It is so criss-crossed by an intricate network of slim canals that from the air it looks like a delicate spider's web. There is so much history - grand palaces where you can marvel at the great heritage of man's creative talents and view the expressive works of Rembrandt and Vermeer. But there is a dark side too, away from the cultural and historical beacons that attract so many tourists. It is one which to my mind makes the waterside capital that started life as a little fishing settlement a sort of spiritual junkyard, in which is gathered the debris of broken dreams and shipwrecked lives from right across Europe.

An environment freed from sexual taboos and restrictive drug-laws, a city priding itself on its liberal philosophy of "live and let others live as they want to", Amsterdam has drawn many people who perhaps only intended to dabble in "a little fun", but then found themselves out of their depth.

Over the years I have visited scores of other major cities all over the world, and there is no doubt that they each have their own poisonous brand of vice, drugs and spiritual oppression wrapped in bright paper to entice the unwary and unsuspecting. But in Amsterdam they seem to be mixed together in particular deadliness.

Here is one of the main arteries of the European drug trade - heroin, cocaine and marijuana almost as freely available as the delicious chocolates for which the Dutch are so renowned. Here is a sex industry so blatant in its publicity that it makes you shudder to think what goes on in secret. Here, too, is a powerful sense of raw evil as occult and weird fringe religions are practised.

Was it really right to risk my life, or more importantly the lives of my precious wife and two young children, to try to reach people with the gospel - people who didn't even seem to care?

As a family we had felt God calling us to live right in the heart of the Red Light District, but waking up most nights at 3 and 4 am to the screams of people being mugged, or the chilling cries of prostitutes fighting with their pimps, wasn't exactly my idea of being a missionary.

Seeing my children struggle with the brutalising effect of living in such an aggressive environment was hard. How could I do this to them as a father who loved them so much? What right had I to expose them and my wife to such scenes of wickedness and depravity? Could God really be in all of this? Or was it all some kind of dreadful mistake?

As I asked myself these questions once more, I reflected back over the years; back to the dusty, dirty streets of downtown New Delhi, India, where it all began.

Two

The Trail

It was an inconsequential encounter, really - but one that triggered a chain of events that changed my life forever. The scorching heat of an early summer's day in 1970 beat down on my wife, Sally, and me as we sat on a park bench in Connaught Circle, a large round park right in the centre of New Delhi. My camera dangled round my neck and we looked much like ordinary tourists watching the stream of people flowing past. A boy, probably in his late teens, walked towards the bench and stopped directly in front of me. He stuck out his hand, palm upturned in that universal gesture of beggars. He certainly looked the part with ragged, filthy clothing, and dirty face and arms. His body was emaciated and his skin stretched tightly across his cheekbones and eye sockets. His eyes were vacant, with an empty look that a doctor sees when his patient is dying slowly by degrees.

The beggars of India! I'd heard about them in a hundred Sunday School classes and sermons, in speeches and essays exhorting people to care about those in need. But nothing can really prepare you for the three-dimensional reality. Now here I was in New Delhi, and here was one of those poor people over whom so many tears were shed back in the comfortable West. Then came the realisation which burst like a bombshell in my mind - this kid was an American! When he took a step closer and begged for money, the language was English and the accent unmistakably middle-American. Here he stood, pitifully begging for a handout on a dusty street in India, thousands of miles from home - barefoot, sick, penniless and with a haunting, jaundiced look in his eyes that said he might never make it back again.

It stunned me to realise that this was an American turned beggar boy. Somehow its impact was like a hammer blow. This young man was not a product of Indian poverty - he did not come to this pathetic condition from a childhood in the back alleys and slums of Bombay, or Delhi, or Calcutta. He came from the land of two-car garages and colour T.V.! The home country of Christian enlightenment, with a church on every corner and a school in every neighbourhood. He came from the nation that boasted the highest standard of living in the history of man - where people died from over-eating, not starvation! A country that sent out missionaries to convert the world.

That was where I came in. Twenty-five years old, with a crew cut, a thin, businessman-type tie, a big Bible, and a deep - though, I was to learn painfully, ill-judged - desire to share with others the God I loved so much. I was here to teach Indian Christians how to reach their fellow countrymen, but somehow the sudden, face-to-face encounter with a lonely, lost American youngster so far from home and so frantically in need of God, jolted me in my well-heeled shoes.

It set me thinking hard; and, looking back, I can see God's hand in it all. I recognised that brief meeting as the first pebble of a landslide that was to follow. At the time, though, I only knew that I was strangely troubled by that young American and as I left the park I could not forget him, could not erase his stark features from my memory.

"What about him, Floyd McClung?" a voice inside seemed to be demanding. "What about him? Don't you care about him? What is he to you? Is he a person to you, Floyd McClung? Does he really matter to you?"

Sally and I stayed in India for a further two months after that - another leg on a busy round-the-world tour as part of a team of young workers from the West - but however busy, I couldn't shake the image that crowded into my mind, of the boy in the park a long way from home.

As we travelled over India that summer, we saw many more young Europeans and Americans like him - hundreds, even thousands, in every major city we visited. The sight became familiar: jeans and backpacks, beads and sandals, beards and long hair - or long flowing dresses. Almost always there were the signs of heavy drug abuse: the spaced-out look, the malnourished body, the watery eyes and runny nose, and the sickness that seemed a constant companion. There were not only Americans, but young people from Australia, Britain, France, Germany, Holland, and a few other Western countries. They called themselves "world travellers" but back home they would have been dismissed as hippies. Their own label was more romantic, more aptly expressive of the nomadic life to which they had turned in search of "something".

They slept out in the parks or on the streets, piled up eight to a room in filthy flophouse hotels, drifting across the country in Land-Rovers that had seen better days, old Volkswagen vans, and ancient buses painted in bright colours and freakish, surreal designs.

As I talked with them, just below that thin epidermis of carefree happiness was a desperate longing to find answers and an almost mystical idealism. For many the search they were on covered up a desperate loneliness and aching emptiness. These were the lost and lonely children of the 60's and early 70's.

They talked of the Trail - the route which wound overland from Europe to India, and over which almost all had travelled. It wasn't marked on any maps or by any road signs, but every drifter in India knew it well. It began in Amsterdam and stretched out across Europe to Athens, Istanbul, across Turkey and Iran, running the length of Afghanistan, through Pakistan, on down into India, and finally up into Katmandu, Nepal.

The Trail was followed by several hundred thousand young people each year. Along the way were cutprice hotels and roadside camps. Drugs were cheap and easy to find and hitch-hikers had little trouble finding a ride.

For many the lure at the end of the road was the romantic, mystical attraction of Eastern religions, the chants and the trances, the robes and bells of unfamiliar rituals, the promise of peace and enlightenment to be found in an ashram - a Hindu temple community - or at the feet of a Buddhist wise man.

But the Trail wasn't kind, and for most it did not fulfil its rich promise. It was filled with hazards unadvertised in the idealistic cities of departure in America and Europe, and as we talked with more and more of the world travellers, the pattern of disillusionment and confusion emerged more clearly and painfully. It easily became a succession of lonely, empty days and nights with no money, shattered idealism and no way of getting home.

The drugs may have been cheap and accessible - but they were also often cut with dangerous substitutes and carelessly mixed, resulting in frequent overdoses and "bad trips". Lice and disease, typhoid, hepatitis and dysentery were constant unwelcome companions. Thieves ran a thriving trade in stolen passports and travellers' cheques, and anyone unfortunate enough to interrupt a burglary might easily collect a knife in his stomach into the bargain!

One girl who had left America three years earlier probably summed it up best of all those we spoke with during those months. She told us: "It's the loneliness that gets to you. People sit alone, staring into space, stoned, not caring. Probably the worst thing, though, is that people stop responding. If you smile at them, they don't know how to react. It's frightening."

We could see how right she was. Even in groups, huddled together over camp fires, many of those young people were desperately lonely. And, in a sad, strange way, many of them were hopelessly lost too. Adrift inside their own heads, they had no values, no goals, no destinations - and no ideas about how to find any.

"You start out on the road and you get sucked into a kind of vacuum," explained a soft-spoken, bearded Californian one day. "You sort of get lost. You get to feel that nothing's important any more - not yourself, or your life, nothing."

As we saw behind their carefree masks, I heard again the voice calling me to account. It whispered: "What are they to you, Floyd McClung? Do you love these kids? These searching, confused kids? These young people who reject you and your ways? Do you care about them - really care about them? Floyd McClung; do you care enough to get involved?"

The awareness that God was speaking to me grew. It became virtually an obsession. I had longed for years for God to break into my life in such a sovereign way that I could not mistake His leading; now I sensed this was it. Our team moved on from India to Africa, and there we encountered more travellers. They, too, talked about the Trail. Though they spoke in idealistic terms, they told of kids sick and stranded in towns like Kabul and Tehran. They spoke of clumsy, crude abortions. They described friends with brains burned out by "acid" and "speed" when they dabbled with drugs once too often, of girls sold into white slavery, and others getting deeper into drugs as depression and loneliness mounted.

They told sadly of acquaintances in Turkish and

Afghan jails, facing long and lonely sentences in squalid, inhuman conditions.. They mentioned the young people who dreamed of and longed for home, but who had lost the will or the means to make the trip back - a journey that was as long and fraught emotionally as it was geographically.

I recognised that these were the lost children of my generation; the idealists who had found only painful, punishing reality - the seekers-after-truth who had hit rock bottom and found themselves spiritually bankrupt. They were alienated, confused and frightened. They had come in search of a dream and woken up in the middle of an unending nightmare.

These were the lost, lonely children of the West - no plastic hippies, no weekend rebels. They weren't just suburban youth running into the city every few weeks to soak up the atmosphere, wear wild clothes, and experiment with a little sex and drugs. These were a different breed. They had gone the whole route - physically, spiritually and emotionally. Drugs, sex, Eastern religion, sometimes smuggling - and now they were twelve thousand miles from home, totally cut off from Western culture and values, and rejecting everything I had always believed in and worked for.

Yet I had the unmistakable conviction that God was calling me to join the Trail - to intercept these young people right where they were, and to reach out to them in love at their point of need. It also seemed to me that I was to do it immediately, permanently, and full-time.

Which, to a straight, never smoked-a-joint "square" like me, with a lovely young wife and dreams of one day having a nice, neat home and a happy little family, seemed to be a perfectly absurd idea.

Three

Believing for the Impossible

By the time we returned to Europe, my resistance to the idea of travelling was weakening. The challenge of taking the message of Christ to the young people following that hazardous route simply would not go away. I was still managing to come up with excuses, but somehow each time I thought of another good one, something in my head shot it down again.

At night I prayed for the young travellers, but I found such intercession to be a pale shadow of the job to which I increasingly knew God was pointing. So I finally decided to tackle the issue head-on - to settle it once and for all. I flew to Lausanne because I wanted to talk with the man who, in a sense, had been my spiritual father. Loren Cunningham was the gifted founder of *Youth With A Mission*, which had its international headquarters at that time in that beautiful lakeside town. He had visited Southern California College while I was a student there and challenged me with the hard, unflinching demands of Christian ministry. I remember clearly sitting in the audience the first time he spoke, electrified by his no-nonsense, enthusiastic approach to evangelism. He encouraged us to believe for the impossible - that we could reach the whole world and every single person with the gospel. He turned things completely around for me, pointing me to the real excitement of a twenty-four-hours-a-day, seven-days-a-week brand of Christianity.

The day after I graduated from college in 1967, Sally and I were married and three days after that we joined the organisation to work full-time together.

Sally and I had then worked under Loren's supervision for four years and I wasn't sure how to tell him what was on my heart. Loren delighted in encouraging others to step out boldly for God, and seeing them blossom and mature as their faith was exercised and developed, but I wasn't sure how he would view my curious burden.

"Loren, I believe that God has something new for me to do," I began hesitantly. Now that the first few words were out it was easier, and I pressed on, eager to share with him the pull I was experiencing. "I've tried to put the idea out of my mind, but it won't go away. God's been speaking to me these past few months about the Hippy Trail. In New Delhi we began to run into literally thousands of Western kids travelling across the East...."

I poured out the whole story almost without drawing breath and told him how I felt God was compelling us to head back across the Trail to India.

Loren cautioned me against leaping ahead, but added that he would support us if we were sure of God's guidance.

"Just make sure, Floyd," he counselled. "Don't make a move until you have specific guidance from the Lord."

Specific guidance - that was the key. As YWAM leaders, we had talked about this many times. It was a concept that may seem naïve to some; that God speaks directly and clearly about important everyday decisions to his disciples. But I had seen it demonstrated clearly dozens of times since joining the organisation, and I was willing to trust my future now to the specific guidance I might receive. I had to know for sure that God was in this, and the only way to find out was to pray for direct confirmation.

As Sally and I waited and prayed, weighing carefully the decision before us, the hazards and pitfalls began to loom larger and larger, and my thoughts became a mingled yarn, with threads of doubt and reluctance lacing the earlier vigorous confidence.

The list of obstacles was lengthy. First there was the question of money - we simply didn't have any! There would be no salary, no support, no organisation or church to pay the bills for a ministry that surely could not pay its own way. Sally and I were willing to live simply, and had done so ever since we were married, but even with that commitment there would be substantial expenses involved in this sort of project. The venture would have to start on faith alone - and while it's no bad resource, it was rather a flimsy commodity when food, fuel, electricity, rent and medical bills fell due.

We would eventually need a base of operations, a place to establish the ministry, but in which country? Many were hostile to missionaries or Christian workers and we couldn't count on them for co-operation in obtaining permission to live permanently within their borders. They would probably be antagonistic to us at times because they would associate us with the young drifters.

My greatest misgivings though concerned my own fitness and suitability for the job. Many of the young people we would be coming into contact with had desperate problems. Amongst them were dope pushers, heroin addicts, thieves, and smugglers. Many were really hardened cases, drop-outs from society who had heard all the sermons and niceties, and rejected them long ago.

What did I have to offer them? I had never smoked a marijuana joint, used cocaine, or shot heroin into my veins. I had never been a radical, never demonstrated against the Vietnam War and never lived in a commune. I seemed so different. But I knew that beyond the externals we shared one fundamental, essential thing - a basic emptiness and a desire for reality that only God could fill. For all our differences, we all needed to stand before our creator as individuals with repentant hearts and hand over all the selfish imperfections of our own lives and step into a new way of living. Through His selfless love for us all He redeemed and reconciled us to Himself. The degree to which we expressed it may have differed; but we had all rebelled against God and needed Jesus to restore that broken relationship.

As a "preacher's kid", I grew up accepting God as a natural part of our lives - the daily Bible readings and family prayers were as much a part of our home as the furniture. I saw God at work throughout the years my father pioneered churches across the States - though I didn't realise at the time that as well as giving me his name he would also pass on his deep desire to see others won for Christ.

Several times we moved as a family - mom, my brother and sister and I - into a small town where dad would take on the pastorate of a struggling congregation or open up a little storefront chapel and go out into the streets to bring people in. When that fellowship was established and thriving, after a few years, we used to pack up our belongings and move on to the next town, where dad would start all over again.

Though I attended church more regularly than many choir boys, I was definitely no little angel. In fact my mother reckons that I went through my teenage rebellion years between the ages of five and ten! Once I threw an old lady's shoes over the edge of a cliff. Another time a friend and I burned down a barn, just to see what would happen! Then there was the occasion I called all the church members and told them they should make every effort to attend the midweek Bible study - it was going to be a special, important meeting.

When dad arrived, he was amazed to find nearly

everyone there, instead of the usual dozen or so. When he found out why they had come - boy did I catch it!

It took someone else to open my eyes properly to God. I was nine years old when a visiting preacher came at dad's invitation to hold a weeklong series of revival meetings at his latest church. When he spoke that night about going to church, reading the Bible and even praying not being enough to make you a Christian - that you had to make your own, personal commitment to Jesus Christ as your Lord and Saviour - I knew he was talking right to me.

At the end of the service, when he made an altar call, I marched right down to the front of that small church in Long Beech, California and gave my heart to Jesus. I wept for a long time as the Spirit of God revealed to me the importance of forgiveness and having a personal relationship with Christ.

I was barely into my teens when I knew that God would one day call me to the mission field. At a Christian summer camp I attended, one of the leaders spoke about how grieved God was that many people in the world didn't know Him, and my heart was broken by the thought that millions of people could die without meeting the Jesus I was growing to love more and more. I pictured a great crowd of people lost without God, and I knew that I wanted to go and tell them how they could find Him. Several years after that I closeted myself away in a room one day with a map of the world, determined not to leave until God had shown me where He wanted me to go.

Several hours later I crept out - tired, thirsty and hungry - none the wiser about my future destination, but with a sense that somehow God was going to use me around the world.

My determination was deepened by that vigil. One day I *would* be a missionary, though I still did not know where or when.

With hindsight it is easy to see that part of the reason

God didn't reveal the specifics of His will at what I considered the appropriate time was that He still had much work to do in preparing me for the future. God had much to teach me, and the person he chose to use in my life at that time was Pop Jenkins.

Seventy-two years old, a five-foot-three, roly-poly grandfather of a figure in a tatty old suit, he introduced himself to me from across my second year study desk at college.

"I've been looking for you," he said simply. "God has called me to serve you. He wants me to be a doormat for you."

I never found out how he knew my name, but our lives became intertwined over the next few months. Something about this almost eccentric old Sunday School teacher fascinated me, and I readily accepted when he invited me to accompany him on a short missionary trip to a small village called San Felipe on the Gulf of Mexico, several hundred miles from my parents' home in Southern California.

From the moment we closed the doors of my old 1947 grey Plymouth and set off on the long haul, he pestered me with the same question, over and over again: "Do you really care?" At first it was something of a novelty. Then it sounded serious and spiritual. Finally it was downright annoying. Every few minutes he said: "Do you really care, Floyd?"

During that trip Pop Jenkins lovingly, gently, but firmly questioned everything - my goals, my values, my motives, my relationships, my insecurities. Why did I want to serve God? Did I truly care about people? What was driving me to enter the ministry?

We stood together in a little cemetery on the top of a hill, looking down on San Felipe. "Christian crosses," he said, pointing at the tombstones. "Religious people, dying without Jesus. Do you really care, Floyd?"

We visited a church service and watched hundreds of poor people as they bowed down before the icon of a dead priest. Without condemnation, tears quietly coursing down his cheeks, he turned to me and asked again: "Floyd, do you really care what happens to people?"

Something inside me began to stir. I cried as I watched him put his arms around a drunken man we met on a dirt road on the edge of the village. As he wept and prayed with this man, introducing him to Jesus, I saw a man who truly cared. I realised that here was someone motivated purely by the love of Christ. Suddenly the irritation I had felt at his constant questioning seemed petty. It was a quiet, thoughtful journey home, but I was alive inside. Pop Jenkins had taken the time and trouble to pour his life into mine, and now a deep longing, an aching desire, had been released within me. I wanted what he had - a concern for people.

As God continued to prepare me for His service there was still a rather unconventional love affair to be fought out. All the struggles of my teen years, when I desperately wanted to run with the pack but was held back by something urging me to stand against it, became focused on the basketball court.

I guess, having long limbs, I was a natural for the game. I really loved it, and took to the sport with a vengeance. In my early and middle teens I practised for up to twelve hours a day, refining and perfecting my skills. I carried a basketball everywhere with me - I even took one to bed! In a perverse kind of way I wanted people to mock or ridicule my zealous commitment, so that I would be spurred on to grit my teeth and steel myself even more to my goal. I'd show them - I was going to be the best basketball player there ever was!

At college I was made captain of the team, and we began a remarkable string of victories against bigger and more well-known university teams from all over the

States. We had one of the highest scoring averages of any college basketball teams, and professional scouts started to follow all our games. There were a few offers from professional teams, and a great deal of adulation and support from friends and the local newspapers.

Then, right in the middle of that winning stretch, God told me to quit the team. It was a choice I knew He had been wanting me to make, but I had managed to push it aside for some time. Now He made it clear in my heart that He wanted to know which came first in my life - Him or this sphere of bright leather filled with air. There was a brief but fierce inner struggle, and finally I gave in.

I immediately walked into a real storm. Team-mates and college friends couldn't believe what I'd done, nor could they understand my reasoning.

They pressurised me and accused me of opting out. I was attacked for being a prima donna and a religious nutcase. It was a tough time, but I knew God was testing me. I didn't want to let the fear of man keep me from putting God first. Unexpectedly, I received most support and understanding through this difficult time from the team coach, Bob Reid. He was a gentle, strong Christian, who understood what the real contest was about. Then, after a few weeks, when the sport had lost its hold on my heart, and I realised how wrong my priorities had been I sensed one day that God was allowing me to play again.

So I hit the courts once more, rejoined the team, and we picked up on our winning ways. But although I still enjoyed playing, it was never the same again. God had set me free from my unhealthy commitment to the game. It had been number one in my life, but now the Lord had taken that place.

Here I was then, several years later, my chin clean-shaven, my hair short, anxious to reach young people who would probably laugh at my seriousness and respectability. My testimony was that of the boy who once smoked half a cigarette and got sick! How could I possibly bridge that gulf to communicate with drug addicts and drop-outs - I who was so drastically different from them; so green, so uninitiated, so inexperienced in the ways of the counterculture?

During my college days, not long after the "Summer of Peace and Love", when San Francisco had been feted in song and in the international media as the beatnik capital of the world, I had spent some time in the city's Haight-Ashbury section - the mecca for America's young radicals and runaways. It was a very different picture from the flowers-in-their-hair peacefulness and tranquility portrayed on T.V. and in the newspapers!

There I had seen youngsters by the score turning off their minds, singing Eastern chants, trying to submit themselves to some vaguely-anticipated religious experience. They craved a mystical event of some kind - any kind - with a pathetic sincerity. They followed the gurus in chanting their "ommm"; their desperation for God's peace was unmistakably real. Those scenes of hopelessness had deeply moved me, and I had departed with a heavy heart.

Now I was faced with the stepchild of the beatniks, the hippy culture, and I wondered if I could cope.

Sally's problem was different; she did not like the Trail. On our YWAM tour she found the poverty overpowering and felt claustrophobic because of the huge crowds of people everywhere she turned. I felt that India was the place the Lord wanted us to settle, but the idea of living there appalled Sally. For three months she prayed and tried to get the matter settled before the Lord and eventually said, "Lord, if that's where You want us, You'll help me to cope." Once Sally had indicated her willingness to obey, she started to look forward to going and had a joy and peace about it.

Her upbringing had been slightly different from mine. She was from Galveston Texas and went to an Assembly of God Church there. Both her parents had been married before and their partners had died leaving them with four children each. When Sally was born, she was at least ten years younger than her half brothers and sisters. It was a grief to her mother that none of the other children were serving the Lord so she and Sally's aunt took the three day old baby to a church, laid her on the altar and prayed that she would grow up to love and serve the Lord and be a missionary. They committed themselves to pray for this every day of Sally's growing years but not to tell her. It wasn't until after we married and had moved in this direction ourselves that Sally's mother told us.

Sally came to the Lord when she was quite young and at the age of five felt the missionary call . When she was older she told the Lord that she wouldn't date non-Christian boys and as a result sat at home on her own most of the time! This resulted in an inner rebellion and struggle which didn't show on the outside but was very real. She lost interest in church activities and knew she was drawing back from what she knew was right, but continued doing it.

What was at first thought to be a bad case of 'flu turned out to be rheumatic fever and Sally was admitted to hospital when she was sixteen. The doctors were worried about permanent damage to her heart as it had gone on so long without being detected. Lying in bed in the hospital, Sally cried to the Lord, "I've made a mess of my life. I've been doing what I wanted, but it hasn't made me happy - I'm sorry, Lord. Please forgive me. I repent of my rebellious attitude and I want to make a fresh commitment to you, Lord."

She realised at that stage that she might be an invalid for the rest of her life, but she wanted to start all over again. She felt a joy and deep happiness, like a fountain bubbling up inside. When the doctors re-examined Sally they found, much to their amazement, that all traces of the rheumatic fever had gone! The Lord not only touched her spiritually, but physically as well - there was no permanent damage at all!

The following Easter, Sally went on a YWAM outreach team to Las Vegas. Now that her life was right with the Lord, she wanted to tell others about Him.

It was on that outreach that Sally and I met. Little did she realise what adventures lay in store for her and the tall, gangly Prince Charming who had charged into her life!

Four

Where He Guides, He Provides

"Where God guides, He provides."
Never had I hoped that spiritual principle would prove to be true more than the day we chugged eastward in our jam-packed Land-Rover. There was no turning back! We could only cling to God's promise, our experience of His absolute faithfulness in times past, and a deep sense that we were doing the right thing.

Once Sally and I were sure of our guidance, we began to put together a team of keen young Christians who wanted to make the trip. During a busy planning and preparation period we spent three weeks staying at a friend's flat near London. We used it as a base from which to tour England, seeking prayer and practical support for the venture. Eventually we had our team, and we set out on our mission proper from YWAM's Swiss headquarters. There were nine of us altogether, a good balance of male and female. With ourselves, all our luggage, and boxes of food and Christian literature crammed somehow into the one vehicle, we ensured that we started the way our work would be continuing - almost living out of one another's pockets! It was a situation for making friends fast. Proof that it is possible to do so is that Gary and Helen Stephens, part of that pioneer team, and now leaders of YWAM's Far East Evangelism Teams and our work in Hong Kong, are still among our close friends.

We made our way slowly and tentatively into Turkey from Istanbul, travelling short distances each day, and gently "feeling our way" into the alternative culture we were entering. We took time to stop and make contacts with other travellers, and picked up hitch-hikers - those that were game to try to squeeze in! We talked with many of the young people, absorbing from them all that we could about the ways of the road. Sometimes we stayed in the hippy hotels that dotted the Trail, often we slept under the open sky.

We were soon intrigued by the lifestyles we observed as we travelled. Stories of free-and-easy drug usage seemed not to have been exaggerated in even the most lurid of popular newspapers back home. Throughout the Middle East we saw morphine, opium, heroin, cocaine and the whole range of psychedelic drugs in heavy and open use. The most commonly-used drug was hashish, which is smoked like marijuana but is much more potent. It was the poor man's high. Hash was as common as drink at a party; virtually everyone smoked it.

All the countries along the route had laws against hashish and other drugs, but enforcement was often an all-or-nothing affair. People who were caught could either get off scot-free or face cruel, harsh jail sentences. It often seemed to depend on no more than how the officials involved had slept the night before! An American radio warning to would-be travellers said: "When you get busted over there, you're in for the hassle of your life."

It was true. Some travellers were thrown into jail and stayed there for months, even years. The award-winning movie of a few years ago, *Midnight Express*, about the experiences in a Turkish jail of Billy Burns, an American youngster arrested for trying to smuggle drugs, paints a grimly realistic picture of what was in store for those who were caught.

During our time in Afghanistan, three young

Americans convicted of smuggling hashish into Turkey from Syria were sentenced to death by firing squad. Their sentences were commuted to life in prison - but what a life! The hippies were so surrounded by drugs in their everyday life that they almost came to forget their illegality. The hit-or-miss attitude of the authorities made it worse; they seemed to be turning a blind eye, then suddenly the axe would fall and there would be summary arrests, harsh sentences, and brutal prison conditions. Travellers were horrified then to find that the Embassies could do virtually nothing to help.

The young Western prison population almost became something of a hidden income for some of the countries along the Trail as prisoners had to provide their own food, or get someone on the outside to do so. The prospects of raising a couple of thousand dollars seemed remote until their very life depended on it, and then relatives and friends back home would sell possessions - cars, and even in some cases homes - to raise the necessary money.

Even with food available, conditions were primitive and squalid. *Midnight Express* didn't overdramatise the awful effects of having to share a dirty cell with up to ten other people - murderers and rapists among them. Brutality and immorality were an integral part of the prison system, involving both officers and inmates.

The full horror was to be summed up by one young American I spoke to shortly after his release from several months inside an Afghan jail. "Under any conditions, doing time in prison is no picnic. But doing time over here is hell. You think sometimes you would be better off dead," he told me emphatically in even, well-measured words.

If tales of jail conditions and sentences were plentiful, so were frightening stories of kidnappings - particularly of young Western girls sold into white slavery by nationals who preyed on the road travellers. We soon learned one of the cardinal rules of the Trail - never let a girl travel alone. The danger was simply too great. Local law officials had little time or sympathy for rape and kidnap victims among the young Western women. They were shocked by the way they flaunted their bodies in their revealing clothes.

As we travelled on, we began to see how thoroughly the pursuit of mystical Eastern religions pervaded the minds and lives of the travellers. It was, after all, why many of them were so far from home in such desolate countries. They were looking for answers in the gurus, the temples, the chants, the philosophies of the East. Like a giant magnet, the religions of Nepal and India drew them along. Some became disillusioned by what they found in the ancient religions; others became true believers, devoting themselves to Krishna, or the teenage Guru Maharaj Ji, or one of the more traditional forms of Hinduism or Buddhism.

We soon discovered how volatile a mix was drugs and mystic religions, both pushing the individual to the borderline that divided illusion from reality. We came across countless young people for whom that distinction was hopelessly, permanently blurred. Hallucinations from drug trips fused with the surreal, emotional philosophy and worship they experienced created hideous distortions in their minds. Some became lethargic and apathetic about even the most routine details of life.

An old Zen saying we heard debated went: "If you fall asleep and dream that you are a butterfly, how do you know when you wake that you are not a butterfly who is dreaming that he is a man?" I saw kids sitting, muddy-brained and confused, inspecting an insect on the ground, pondering such questions for days on end, turning the issue over and over inside their heads like a simple-minded child.

At the root of the heavy drug abuse, the sexual

hedonism and the pursuit of Eastern mysticism lay a profound sense of alienation from Western culture. The long hair and beads, the flowing hippy clothing, and the loose, low-key, laid-back lifestyle were all symbols of their rejection of everything associated with the pressure-filled, materialistic society they saw as being life back home. They maintained they were retiring from the rat race, leaving aside all the hypocrisy and the puritanical values, and pressure to conform and compete. They endeavoured to leave behind the civil service, the MA and the PhD, the mortgage in the suburbs, the neat nuclear family, and the nine-to-five rut.

By setting off on the Trail, they were leaving behind the Church - and the stale, empty lies which to them it perpetrated.

Two stereotypes of Christianity seemed to dominate their thinking. One was the "believer-as-hypocrite"; giving lip-service to Christ in the pew on Sunday, but never really living it. Talking about love and morality, but living immorally; shaking the preacher's hand at the door on the way out of church and then roasting him as assuredly as the chicken or lamb enjoyed at home a little later. Then there was the other archetypal Christian - the "disciple-as-fanatic". The wild-eyed Bible banger, grabbing unsuspecting people by the lapels and force-feeding them the gospel; full of dramatic answers and wonderful testimonies, but never having time to listen to the questions.

So we had all that to overcome. We began simply by listening, watching, learning, straining to hear and perceive what these disaffected young people were saying. Gradually we began to understand the perspective from which they were viewing the world they had left behind. Slowly they began to recognise that we were there to love them, not to preach at them in a sermonising way to put them down, not to cluck our tongues and wag our heads at their depravity, but to love them and to tell them about Jesus Christ, Who loved them before we did.

Clocking up miles and experience, we became more aware of the travellers' world. It was fascinating. While driving overland though, I realised that I wasn't absolutely sure that India was the place for us to settle - but we headed in that direction trusting that the Lord would reveal to us what was right.

From Istanbul to Ankara we travelled, onto Erzurum and the Turkish-Iranian border, Tehran and Meshed, then into Afghanistan. Then through the bleak, foreboding deserts of Afghanistan to Herat, Kandahar, and finally Kabul!

Afghanistan is one of the fiercest countries in the world - as well as one of the most primitive, with sixty per cent infant mortality and ninety-four per cent adult illiteracy. It was like going back into history 2000 years. People carried guns as naturally as they would drive cars at home. An ancient Eastern fable says that when Lucifer was cast down from heaven, he fell into Kabul. In all the world there was no country so rugged, so stark and frightening to Western eyes as Afghanistan. And all of that wild land was reflected in Kabul, concentrated in a city of three hundred thousand people - today swollen to three times that with refugees from the fighting that has waged since the Russian invasion.

Even after several weeks on the Trail, we were still not prepared for what we found there. Called "the crossroads of Asia", the city was also the bottleneck of the hippy trail. There was more than one route from Istanbul across the East to India, but all paths converged at Kabul, situated as it is at the mouth of the famous Khyber Pass, that narrow gap through the Hindu Kush Mountains that all world travellers had to take. Over the mountains lay Pakistan, India and Nepal and all the promises of the land of the

Hindus. And there, at the foot of the mountains, guarding the rocky gateway like a squat, squalid sentry, was Kabul.

We stayed there for several days, making contact with another busy team of young YWAM-ers, led by Lynn Green. They were working in the city on a special outreach mission during the summer months, attempting to make contacts with some of the Western visitors. Although we were eager to move on to India, we were somehow arrested by the enormous needs of the swarm of young people in Kabul. The city virtually overflowed with sick, stranded, strung-out young people; it seemed to have collected the have-nots of the entire Trail - the down-and-outs who had exhausted their money, their health, or their emotional stamina, and who could go no further. Kabul was the sick bay of the Trail, but there were hardly any medical staff to take care of all the patients. It was teeming with thieves and rip-off artists who stole money and passports from young people too stoned or weak to resist.

There were dozens of hippy hotels - little more than hovels - crammed with people too ill, wiped-out or penniless to move on. Drugs were cheap and plentiful - pharmacists sold morphine shots over the counter for a few pennies. The best hashish in the East could be had for less than 25 afghanis, the price of a bar of chocolate in the West.

For all its size, Kabul had no water-filtration plant, and with little resistance to the high bacterial levels, scores upon scores of Western youngsters contracted typhoid and dysentery. Hepatitis from dirty needles was common, too, and Afghan hospitals could be worse than none at all. Psychiatric patients still had their heads routinely shaved as in Medieval times!

The Kabul police arrested so many travellers that they kept a separate prison for foreigners. Travellers died of overdoses in their hotels, and there were reports that they were sometimes buried secretly in the desert by hotel operators, who preferred not to have the inconvenience of officially reporting the death.

Amid all of this there was no-one to care, no-one to be alarmed. These victims of the savage, unglamorous realities of Kabul life were thousands of miles from home; often with parents not knowing where they were. They were lonely, and they were lost in the shuffle, and if they made it home, or to the next stop along the way, then that was fine. Equally, if they didn't that was OK too.

We reeled under the emotional intensity of it all. On the one hand, we felt drawn to this strange and wonderful place. Was it possible that God wanted us to stay here? If so, He would have to make it very clear. In Kabul we saw all the miseries of the Trail compressed violently and painfully into a single city, and the impact was staggering.

Five

A Rude Awakening

As we prepared to leave Kabul and rush on to India, I was approached by Dr. Christy Wilson. He was pastor of the Kabul Community Christian Church - the only Christian church in the entire country - and almost a legend throughout Afghanistan. His church served the Westerners of Kabul - the diplomats and personnel, business executives and engineers who lived in the city.

It had been at his prompting that the short-term YWAM teams had worked in the city for two consecutive summers, and now he told me: "Floyd, this town is in urgent need of a permanent ministry to all these world travellers. These kids need someone to minister Jesus to them - you can see how desperate their problems are." I certainly could. "Stay here in Kabul," he urged. "Set up a house that will provide help for them, and my congregation will support you with our prayers, help, and whatever money we can."

That night Sally and I prayed about what Dr. Wilson had said, and as we did so I sensed firmly the inner whisper: "This is the second prophet of the dream you had months ago. Listen to him." While in Canada I had had a simple dream of two men who I knew instinctively were prophets. Nothing dramatic happened in the dream, but I saw two men of God and heard a voice which said: "Don't listen to the first prophet - wait for the second." I was puzzled as I reflected on this: I am not the sort of person to jump in and say, "The Lord gave me a dream," and I was cautious about attributing any meaning to it. As time went by, though, I had a growing sense that the dream was of some significance. I prayed that if it did mean something special the Lord would make it clear to me.

When I got back to Europe after our world tour, a man of God I loved and respected made me an offer. As I prayed about it, I felt the Lord saying to me: "This is the first prophet in your dream," so although I was very flattered I turned it down.

Now here in Afghanistan was the second prophet of my dream, but was I absolutely sure? All the time the face of the young American beggar boy in India had been in front of me, so India had seemed the obvious place for our ministry. I had to be sure about the change in direction and position. I needed further guidance, so I gathered Sally and the rest of the team together, and we prayed for God to give us specific and clear direction from His Word. As I went to bed that night, He impressed upon me a passage - Ezra chapter one, verses two and three. I turned to it with anticipation:"... and He has appointed me to build a temple for Him...." Next morning, one of the girls in the group came to me; she had been praying the night before to ask for direction for the team and God had given her a verse of Scripture.

"What was the passage?" I asked.

"The first three verses of Ezra," she told me. "I looked it up straight-away. It's something to do with building the house of God." It was exactly the same verse God had given me. Coincidence? No way!

We praised God for this double confirmation of His will. We felt sure that He was telling us through this brief passage to build a house of the Lord - not literally, of course, but to establish a ministry that could help the

needy young people in Kabul. We agreed to test this
guidance still further by going on to India as planned, but
as we travelled to New Delhi there was no peace in our
hearts and the conviction grew in us daily that God
wanted us in Kabul so we turned the Land-Rover round
and headed back.

Sally and I were certain now that God had guided us to
Kabul - and now it was up to Him to provide the means,
because we arrived back almost penniless. Two or three
other team members also felt they should stay in Kabul
and join our work, even if only temporarily. The
remainder of the team returned to Europe. We pooled
what little cash we had left and that night we prayed for
God to keep us afloat.

We set up quarters in the Olfat Hotel, in the heart of the
hippy district downtown. The earlier YWAM team had
used the fifth and sixth floors of the small hotel during the
summer, and we took it over from them as they left.
Actually, the description "hotel" may give a rather
misleading impression - the Olfat was considerably better
than most of the other crude places used by the travellers,
but to Western eyes it was more of a shabby warehouse
than a hotel. The "bedrooms" consisted simply of a small,
bare chamber occupied by just a rough "char-pai" - a
wooden frame held together by a rope mat, with a blanket
thrown on top to act as a mattress.

That first morning, after Bible-study sessions and the
chores of the house were completed, we formed a circle on
the floor. Sitting on large, striped Afghan rugs, with flies
buzzing about us and the sounds of trucks, camels and
shouting people drifting up from the streets below, we
prayed for the kids we were going to meet.

On the fifth floor of the Olfat we made our living
quarters, and the entire sixth floor, at the top of the
building, was occupied by a tea-house. Coffee was
virtually unknown in the East and the common drink in

Afghanistan was tea, known as "chai" in the Farsi language. Our strategy at the outset was simply to operate a "chai house" in the evenings, giving us an opportunity to get alongside and talk with the young travellers. We made contact with them by going out onto the streets during the day to visit their flophouse hotels, which were run-down, flea-infested places, and inviting them along for free chai and conversation.

Everyone was welcome, no questions asked. But for those young people who were really serious about learning more about Christianity, we had some unoccupied bunks. On a selective basis, we invited them to stay with us and study the Bible. Many hours were spent discussing the meaning of life, philosophical questions and political issues. We challenged them to watch our lives, live among us, and then make their own decision about the claims of Jesus.

The Olfat was located just off Chicken Street, a long narrow thoroughfare that was the main route of the hippy district. On one side of the building was an open "park" - mostly just dirt - and on the other was an open-air bazaar. All along Chicken Street were small shops which sold clothes, incense, drugs, food and - as you may guess - lots of chickens. At one end, just around the corner, was "Sigi's". This restaurant was run by a German, and it boasted a lingering smell of hashish which practically intoxicated anyone just walking through the door! It was the most popular traveller's haunt in the city. All down Chicken Street and the side streets that ran into it were the rough hippy hotels with names like the Najib, Noristan, Hindustan, Peace Hotel and Bandamir.

On the first day I pushed open the little wooden door at the gate of the Bandamir. It opened into a big courtyard, where I saw sleeping bags spread around on the ground, and several char-pais scattered around. Youngsters were lying all over the ground, some leaning up against the walls, stoned. Some were quietly smoking hashish through chillams, Afghan water pipes. Over against a far wall, under a stunted tree, sat four guys just looking at each other - nodding pitifully under the effect of the drugs; they were too glassy-eyed and spaced-out to talk to each other. Their clothes were filthy, and their teeth yellow and scummy.

I sat down beside another young American, who was mumbling half-coherently to himself, and tried to strike up a conversation with him, but it was impossible. He turned his head slowly in my direction, looked at me blankly, and then went on talking to himself.

In another corner of the yard was a tall, dark-haired Frenchman - a few solitary hairs dangled from his chin to mark an unsuccessful attempt to grow a beard. He had a thin, bony face, with sunken eyes, but in Indian pants and a loose, blousy shirt, his appearance was somehow striking. My eyes fixed on him, in morbid fascination, as he placed a candle on the ground and lit it, deftly wrapped a tourniquet around his wiry bicep, poured a little water into a dirty, bent-up spoon, and dropped a morphine tablet into it. As it cooked, he searched for a protruding vein on his arm to shoot into. Finally he found a spot on the back of his wrist, drew the milky coloured solution into a hypodermic needle, and plunged it into the vein. He waited for the "rush" - the jolt of the morphine - to hit him. When it didn't come, he swore violently with dissatisfaction, muttering angrily at the impotence of the "junk". He sat down next to the wall to enjoy the trip for whatever he could salvage from it.

I walked over, sat down beside him, and introduced myself. I was still flushed and trembling, my heart racing, at what I had witnessed. For all the movies and talk, I had seen someone "shoot up" for the first time, and I struggled hard to hide the fact that I was deeply shaken by the whole scene.

The Frenchman, Jacques, looked me over without saying a word. He scrutinised me from head to toe, from my Marks & Spencer shoes to my close-cropped hair. Instantly he could see that I was nervous and on unfamiliar territory, that I didn't belong there in the Bandamir courtyard and that I was from a different place and culture. A whole different world from his.

He looked straight into my eyes as I told him about the chai house, and invited him to come over and to bring his friends. Then he laughed, looked at me again, now with contempt and disdain showing on his features, and laughed again.

With soul-baring discernment he proceeded to tell me who I was and where I stood; he tore me to shreds. I was green and raw, he declared. I knew nothing about these kids, had no concept of what made them the way they were, what drove a young person from the middle-class American suburbs halfway round the world to a Hindu ashram. He swept an arm contemptuously across the courtyard scene, gesturing towards the nodding, zombie-like youngsters strewn across it. What did I know of this life? How could I possibly hope to help them with a few Bible verses and a cup of tea?

Seeing that I was stunned, on the defensive and unable to begin to argue with him, he bore down harder. He questioned me about my personal life, my background, my reasons for being there. He laughed at my innocence and naïvete, my obvious uncertainty.

I sat transfixed as he talked, able only to attempt the occasional feeble response. Finally he closed the exchange with a parting comment that cut deeper than all his previous, knowing wounds. He looked at me solemnly - almost sadly - and said evenly, in judgement: "You'll never help anybody!" I swallowed hard, as he added: "And you're a fool for being here."

Chastened and heartsick, I left the cluttered courtyard

and returned wearily to the Olfat where I hid myself in the little bedroom Sally and I shared and turned to God in prayer with a deep feeling of despair. I knew that Jacques had been right. He had seen me more clearly than I had seen myself - how inadequate I was, how out of place. His final words rang in my ears, and for a few moments, as I looked around the empty room, while the sounds of a strange, grim culture floated up through the windows, I agreed with him.

As I prayed, God taught me an important lesson through my painful experience that first morning in Kabul. "To reach these young people," He seemed to tell me, "you must identify with them; you must become one with them." He reminded me that I must step into their world and that as I did so, He would give me what I lacked. He would give me the ability to identify and relate - to be a real friend, which would make all the difference.

This spiritual principle of identification is essential if we are to make meaningful, effective contact with others - be that in the sophisticated, pressurised cities of the West, or the remote parts of the under-developed Third World. It means becoming one with people in the way that Jesus became one with mankind. He left His home and came alongside us to experience and align Himself with all that we face. Just as the cross could never have happened if Jesus hadn't become one of us - born a baby, grown into a man - so I am convinced that the message of salvation can never be truly meaningful or understood by any individual or group of people until we take the gospel and flesh it out first, in and through our own lives. Just like Jesus did.

Jesus was known as the friend of sinners. He spent time with people, He knew their names, their worries and their dreams and ambitions. Yet there was no compromise in Him. He was a friend of sinners, but He did not enter into their sins. In the same way, we should become one with those we live and work with without losing our integrity and our fundamental commitment to God's truth. In the right time and place, we must lovingly confront our friends with the claims that God and His kingdom make on their loves. It is not an easy task. It means becoming so close to people that we hurt with them - even weep with them - but never lose our sense of balance; never becoming so emotionally involved with someone or caught up in his problems that we cannot challenge him with the truth.

Such involvement is only made possible as we love people with honesty and genuineness. Identification means giving up our rights, laying down our reputation but doing it so that we can present people with the truth of Christ. Nowhere is this spoken of more beautifully than in Philippians chapter two, where we are told that Jesus "did not consider equality with God something to be grasped, but made Himself nothing, taking the very nature of a servant...."

God began to teach me this painful but essential truth in a Kabul courtyard - with a little help from a Frenchman named Jacques! There were times afterwards when I did the wrong thing, when I failed miserably, but never again did I doubt that my place was in Kabul. From that moment on, I knew that I could minister to drug addicts, even though I had not taken drugs. I'd had my rude introduction to the realities of the task that faced us, the demands and changes it would require. I knew that the job was going to be far more difficult than I had ever imagined - but I was equally convinced that by His enabling grace, through the power of the Spirit, we could love and identify with the people God had called us to reach.

I found it easy to adapt to the hippy style of dress. To me, it was fun and I enjoyed wearing the loose, baggy Indian clothes, beads and obligatory long hair and beard, which of course took time to grow. Others on our team dressed in the style of clothes they had always worn and were loved and accepted for who they were.

Sally never regarded herself fully as hippy or straight. She wore a mixture of western and eastern clothes and it became a joke that her hippy clothes were clean and ironed - a marked contrast to some of the others! She was willing to obey the Lord but felt that she didn't need to conform outwardly to the hippy style of dress if she wasn't comfortable with it. If she had tried to be something she was not, those we were working with would have realised straight-away - their sensitivity made it easy for many of them to sense a phoney person.

In the end, Sally was accepted for who she was. After many months of struggling, she accepted that her identity came from the inside, not from her appearance.

With a new confidence I returned to the Bandamir to invite Jacques once more to the Olfat. I went straight to his room, bolder than before, determined to make another attempt to win him over. As I opened the door, I was assaulted by a strong smell of hashish. The room was crowded with people, mostly sitting around the walls on char-pais. As before, everyone was stoned except Jacques. Several people were passing joints back and forth, and the walls were covered with grotesque paintings. From the ceiling hung a long, twisting piece of flypaper, covered with dead flies.

Jacques was squatting on the floor, and to my surprise he greeted me warmly; perhaps pleased that I had come back, perhaps just glad to see a fresh face amid all the trance-like expressions in the room. He introduced me to his girlfriend, Shirley, a pretty clean-looking young Californian who was wearing a thin Indian blouse. She was kneeling beside him as he taught her how to sniff cocaine.

He interrupted his endeavours, gestured to me to sit down, and we talked. This time the conversation was different, and by the time I had left the mood had changed. Jacques had promised to drop in at the Olfat with Shirley. To me at that time, it was the crossing of a huge hurdle. I had begun to identify with Jacques and those like him. The compassion of the Holy Spirit had started to flow from me to them and God had given me that special sensitivity which I had prayed for, to meet them where they were and to communicate effectively.

As it turned out, we would all have been better off if Jacques had laughed in my face again that second time.

From his first visit to the Olfat a few days later, Jacques was a disruptive force - a smooth, slick-talking, persuasive operator, who talked of his abhorrence of drug pushers while selling drugs to the very kids in our place who were trying to kick their habits. Suave and seductive, he visited our chai house often that first month, talking of his interest in our faith just enough to keep us welcoming him back, but never making a really serious move towards Jesus.

Sadly, we were taken in by him, and allowed him to hang around. Eventually, we discovered that Jacques had been a big-time pusher all along, even hiring young French lads to operate a drug-and-theft ring from the Bandamir. He had connections, knew every thief in town, and dealt also in stolen passports and travellers' cheques. The police finally raided his room - but Jacques had moved out just a few hours before, and escaped the country.

Six

Sheep with Sharp Teeth

That first month in Kabul we were plagued by wolves in sheep's clothing. We were gullible, plain and simple. So determined were we to be loving and accepting, so eager to reach people with the gospel, that we were vulnerable to being manipulated and deceived. Many feigned interest in our talk of Jesus - at times claiming they had accepted Him as their Saviour - to get food and attention, or maybe just a roof over their head. They drained our already meagre resources and were not genuinely interested in the gospel as they pretended, but blocked us from extending ourselves to others in need.

We made mistakes in our novices' enthusiasm, but I believe that the flood of tricksters who made our early days so difficult cannot be attributed solely to inexperience. Rather, I firmly believe that Satan was jealous for his unchallenged position in Kabul, and determined so to swamp us with trouble that we would be discouraged, defeated, and sent home with our tails between our legs. There were times when we came close to it.

I hadn't always believed so positively in a literal, active Devil. In earlier years I had viewed Satan more as an abstraction than as a personal reality, a being of power and cunning. But his absolute reality was just one of the lessons we learned on the travellers' trail. Away from the stained-glass, complacent life of the American and British churches, we saw Satan at work in raw, naked struggles for the lives of young people. I am convinced about his individual existence, and I'm sure that he was personally infuriated by our arrival in Kabul.

Many times en route to Afghanistan we had heard stories from reliable friends of great miracles wrought by Hindu and Krishna worshippers. Such accounts were legion on the Trail, and they made convinced Hindu believers of thousands of young people. Hindu priests were observed walking three inches above the ground, or stepping barefoot across beds of fire without discomfort or injury. Mystics had themselves padlocked into a bare room without food or water for up to forty days. Then they would walk out in the best of health and tell accurately of events which had occurred in distant towns during their confinement. They explained that, by the power of Krishna, they had separated their souls from their bodies, which had then travelled freely about.

A young Irish lad named Rick, a self-confident philosophy student, came to the Olfat during the first few weeks. He had been in an Indian ashram - a meditation centre - studying under the acclaimed guru, Sri Baba. He told how he had been an agnostic until he witnessed great healings and miracles performed by the guru, who claimed to be the tenth Avatar, or reincarnation, of God Himself. Rick now believed, he said, because he had seen these incredible events with his own eyes, and only the true God could work such wonders. Being himself truly convinced, Rick was a persuasive spokesman for the guru, and he created enormous doubt and confusion among our already-confused visitors when he called in.

Were such miracles real? Undoubtedly, I am sure that Rick spoke honestly as he related his tales of healings and miracles. But if they were real, what was their source? The Bible teaches that Christians must learn to distinguish between that which is evil and that which is good. There is a dimension of life that is spiritual in nature, and its power supersedes that of the temporal reality we observe with our senses. In this spiritual realm there are forces at work, some of them evil and some good.

Again and again we observed Satan and his power at work. The Bible declares that Satan is the source of evil power and he is not to be taken lightly. He works his own miracles and seeks to deceive and confuse. To the strung-out, experience-oriented seekers in Kabul, these evil-inspired miracles were powerful arguments indeed.

The addicts brought us other problems. One such was Chris, a Belgian junkie. He was good-looking, dandily-dressed, and fluent in four languages, and although hooked on morphine, he was meticulously clean - almost compulsively sanitary. Everything had to be perfect for him - he kept a special needle and syringe kit, always spotless and sterilised, used only distilled water and never shot up in front of people. He thought he could quit the drugs any time he wanted to.

Chris was interested in a girl who was coming to us for help, so he feigned an interest in our work, saying he wanted us to help him get off morphine. But right from the start his attitude was condescending and arrogant. He was our first hardline addict, and he knew it. His game was to shoot secretly, while outwardly he pretended to be coming off drugs as we all sweated and struggled to help him.

We were beginners at the junkie game, and he was a seasoned drug user, a veteran con artist. He gave us a one-man education in the way of addicts, lessons that I haven't forgotten to this day.

He would beg to go outside, swearing not to try to make a "connection" with a dealer. I would refuse to let him go, and he would storm and rail convincingly at me: "Don't you trust me? Can't you see I'm going straight? I'll never touch the stuff again!" And all the time he had syringes, needles and morphine tablets secreted all over the premises.

Perversely, Chris also lectured us on how to screen addicts and how to keep them from deceiving us. He taught us never to allow them to get mail, which could let crushed morphine powder into the place, and to watch them wherever they went when they were alone, since they might have hidden drugs somewhere. All the time he was giving us golden rules by which to help addicts break their habits, he was quietly maintaining his habit on the sly.

Finally he left the Olfat and returned to his hotel, threatening to commit suicide if I didn't go over and get him. "I've got enough morphine in this needle to kill two men," he screamed at me over the 'phone. "If you don't come and get me now, I'll overdose and kill myself right here!" But when I told him that the girl he had been pursuing at the Olfat was no longer with us, he lost interest, disappeared, and soon left Kabul. We learned valuable lessons from Chris, but at the cost of considerable turmoil and disruption that gripped the place while he was around.

Of all the deceivers who came our way, though, Patsy was the most frightening, and perhaps the most powerfully used by Satan. She came from a wealthy Chicago home, and had spent some time in India. Initially when she came to the chai house, she expressed an interest in what we had to tell her about Jesus, and stayed around. But we learned later that she was at the same time the leader in the Kabul occult scene, conducting regular seances and Black Magic ceremonies. Unknown to us, she even introduced some of the young people she met at the Olfat to her occult practices.

Patsy was a witch - a full-blooded tool of the Devil. She had long, blonde hair, and had used her good looks to lure many young men into her bed. She demonstrated a classic multiple personality of the "Three Faces of Eve" variety. One moment she seemed congenial and pleasant, and the next she seemed to have changed personalities entirely. Once she practically went berserk, and was locked into a small room at the Mustafa Hotel, where she was staying, by fearful staff. She emerged from that locked room with strange teeth marks clearly visible on parts of her body inaccessible to her own mouth.

We had a table tennis table at the chai house, and one night Patsy started a game with Marti, one of our team members. Each rally between the players lasted for six strokes of the ball, and Patsy, with what Marti later described as "a weird, sick grin on her face", would call out the number six. It happened time after time - six hits of the ball, no more, no less. And over and over again, Patsy would intone monotonously: "Six...six...six...six..." Something about the incident was strange and troubling, and Marti became very upset, frightened and unable to go on with the game.

That night in our group devotions, Marti felt that God was impressing her with a Bible reference for us all. Such leading was not uncommon, so we all waited while she turned to the appropriate verse. It was Revelation chapter thirteen, verse eighteen, and the colour drained from her face as she read it aloud. We all became quiet and grim, as Marti read: "This calls for wisdom. If anyone has insight, let him calculate the number of the beast, for it is man's number. His number is six-six-six."

We prayed for Patsy urgently. She told one of the young converts who was staying with us that she had cast a spell on him, and that he would have to die if she was to continue to live. The German boy was very anxious, and became depressed and morbid. He grew obsessed with the idea of his own death, and made a serious suicide attempt - in a twisted, convulsive way, the spell seemed to be working.

It was decided that something had to be done, so a group of our team went to find Patsy. They were led by Lynn Green, who was due to return to Europe soon himself, after leading the YWAM summer team. Now Lynn heads the YWAM work across Europe, but then he was still a young Christian himself, having been saved a couple of years previously. In a comparatively short time, however, he had proved himself to be a man of great faith and power with God.

When they got to the Mustafa Hotel, Lynn knocked on Patsy's door. No answer. He pushed it open, and there inside was Patsy. She was lying on the bed, naked and stoned out of her mind. The group quietly gathered round her, covered her with a sheet, and then Lynn prayed, imploring the Holy Spirit to drive out the evil spirits within her, rebuking the demons, and binding Satan and his work in her life.

Patsy did not return to the Olfat after that, and the fear she had struck and stirred in people's hearts disappeared. A few weeks later, her concerned parents finally located her, and through the American embassy in Kabul wired her enough money for the air ticket home. Embassy staff urged her to go back to her parents, and when she refused to listen, they asked me to persuade her.

"Look," I told her, "let's not play any more games. I know what you are, and you know what you are. You're sick, and you need help. You're being taken advantage of by every Afghan man that comes along, and it's breaking your body down. You're going to die if you stay around this town much longer! So how about getting on that plane and getting out of here?"

Patsy looked up at me from her bed with a spaced-out, wild grin. Then she snarled at me, hostility spitting from her eyes, as she told me to mind my own business.

But I had one more question. It was direct and to the

point: "Patsy, do you know Lynn Green?"

With that, a cold, frightened look fell over her face. Her tone changed instantly, and she muttered something too low and subdued for me to understand very well. I left the room. When an embassy official came to the hotel the following morning, Patsy was ready to leave Kabul.

But, to her parents' further distress, not to return home. When her plane made a refuelling stop in Athens, she got off, gave her ticket to a West-bound hippy who happened to be at the airport, and disappeared into the Greek interior.

Many times during those first months we felt like packing up and going home. Some of our original team members had had to leave because of other commitments. They were replaced by new and willing workers, so we always had people to pray and share with, but as leaders Sally and I felt the discouragements more deeply than they did. In spite of everything, though, we knew we had to stay.

Seven

The Dysentery Daily

We had always felt that our home would play an important role in our work and this was confirmed when we spent a month at the L'Abri Fellowship in Switzerland, where we spoke to Francis and Edith Schaeffer and other L'Abri workers before embarking on the Trail. The Schaeffers had learnt to open their home to searching young people and our time spent with them was an inspiration to us.

Learning from the Schaeffers' example, Sally in particular felt that no matter how simple the furnishing or decoration, a home should be a testimony of who God is and although at that time Edith Shaeffer's book *Hidden Art* had not been published, we adapted many of the L'Abri principles to fit in with our somewhat different circumstances - Swiss chalets to flophouse hotel! At the Olfat we had very basic furniture - pillows or mats on the floor for sleeping on and simple chairs made of either wood or straw - but we had candles and fresh flowers on a clean table cloth when we ate our communal meal. Sally wanted the table to be a reflection of beauty and order; to express simply the character of God.

Although Sally was very involved with the people we were helping, she felt her major role was that of homemaker and over the years this developed so that she became an expert in interior design.

The principle on which we had launched our family-style living in Kabul was that no-one would ever be paid for their work. We would receive food and shelter, but everyone would be expected to share equally in the responsibility of "praying in" enough money to keep the bills paid and the grocery cupboard full. We had no church supporting us back home in the States, and there was no-one in the team gainfully employed. Whatever income we received would result from prayer - coming unsolicited, as God moved His people to give. God had led us into a situation where we had to learn to live by faith. In those days He taught us that the spiritual realm truly does have authority over the temporal - that He could provide for our practical needs even in the middle of a desolate and remote place like Afghanistan. Those lessons of faith became spiritual foundations that have served us ever since.

Almost no-one outside Kabul knew about our work, and through the help of many dear friends in the Kabul Christian Community Church we made it through more than a few tight spots. In this way we discovered what it means to live "by fellowship" with our Christian brothers and sisters, as well as by faith. We were amazed to see God answering prayers from both near and far. One particular bolt-from-the-blue experience that touched us deeply involved a young girl staying with us who had been challenged by my request that each person accept an equal responsibility for praying in the money needed. However, no-one who knew her back home had any idea where she was at the time.

Despite her reservations, she decided to take the plunge, so she came to me and said that she wanted to become a full-fledged member of our Olfat "family", and that she would take on the task of praying in her contribution each month. To underline how serious she was, she handed over all the money she had with her, about 5,800 afghanis, which is equivalent to one day's wages for a secretary today. Recognising her commitment, I prayed that God would honour her trusting step by demonstrating clearly His generous provision.

The next week a miraculous improbability occurred that confirmed her decision. She drove to the post office with Sally and among the letters was one from a friend in Portugal with whom she had not been in contact for nearly a year. Inside the envelope was the exact amount of her monthly prayer pledge - with the simple note: "I just got a burden last week to send you this money. God bless."

Sitting in the car outside the post office that day, they praised God for His goodness and love. For the non-Christians who were living with us our dependence upon God for daily provision and His miraculous supply was a powerful testimony to God's reality.

He also met our needs in the serious problem of manpower. We badly needed a cook, and a native Afghan who could shop at the market and bazaar and find bargains that would simply be beyond the scope of an uninitiated foreigner.

We happened to mention this need to a friend from the community church. That same week while shopping in one of Kabul's open air markets, she spotted an Afghan called Ishmael, who at one time had worked in the kitchens in some of Kabul's finest diplomatic residences. She stopped him and asked him where he was working. "Nowhere," he responded, a little embarrassed. A few days previously he had finished working for a Westerner who was leaving the city, and had not found suitable new work yet. Our friend hired him for us on the spot! Ishmael proved to be a real blessing. He was clean, honest, and a great market-haggler, bargain hunter and cook. He worked for well below what he could have earned in other places - but when offered posts elsewhere he responded that he liked working with us because there was an atmosphere of love and peace.

Another pressing personnel need in the early days in Kabul was for a multilingual secretary who could speak the various languages of the road. We were at a loss, because certainly none of the original members of the team could handle such a job. As we were discussing the need, we received a call from a tourist in the city who was sick and needed a doctor. Her name was Hellen. She was a Dutch Christian, and in addition to speaking French, Italian, Hebrew, Portugese and Spanish, she was a secretary. Needless to say, we challenged her to stay on with us as part of the team - which she did.

Soon it became abundantly clear to us that one of the greatest needs among the drop-out community of Kabul was the services of trained medical staff. We wanted to start a free clinic, so that we could help travellers who got sick along the way, and present the claims of Jesus on their lives to them as well. We had a registered nurse, Jeanette Boteler, on the team, but although she could maintain such a clinic fairly well once it was operational, she couldn't start one up. That needed the specific skills and expertise of a doctor, and there was little prospect of our coming across one.

So God blew one in out of nowhere. Richard Winter was as surprised to find us in Kabul as we were to meet someone like him. Now a psychiatrist and counsellor with the British L'Abri team, he was then a recently-qualified doctor who looked more like a typical world traveller than many of the young people themselves, and certainly more like a hippy than a doctor!

He and his new wife, Jane, who were both Christians, had decided to travel for a year before settling down, and had trekked through Central and South America, across Africa, and into India. As they worked their way backwards along the Trail from India and through Nepal,

Richard was moved by the emptiness of the Eastern religions in which so many young people were earnestly seeking truth, and their immediate medical needs. He had resolved to help them if he ever got the opportunity.

Arriving in Kabul, a friend suggested that the Winters stay with us at the Olfat, and from the moment they walked in through the door it seemed almost too good to be true. We immediately made our case for a free clinic at the Olfat, and openly and forthrightly asked him to stay and start one for us. Richard said that he wasn't absolutely sure. He needed to be certain that the need was great enough to justify such a commitment. So the next day he went out onto the streets to see if conditions in Kabul warranted his staying on.

He went first to a hotel just down the street from our chai house - and I believe that God led him to just the right door. In that first room he entered lay four young men, each of them deathly sick with amoebic dysentery. Too weak to move, badly in need of medical attention, they could only lie there in their own filth.

That was enough for Richard and Jane. They unpacked their bags and stayed with us for a vital few weeks to found our free clinic. We opened up the very next day, in an empty storeroom at the Olfat. There was no sophisticated equipment. Richard had his little black bag, I gave him a small flashlight, and we hung a picture of Jesus on the wall. The surgery was open.

Much of the work was basic but vital. He taught us simple health care that we were able to pass on to the travellers, and he supervised the treatment with the few medicines we had - some kaolin and morphine, and a few dysentery tablets. For the very sick there were some intravenous fluids available, and Richard's skills were essential. He also helped us launch a small news-sheet of tips for the travellers, which we gave away in the streets and at the hotels. *The Dysentery Daily*, as we called it, advised how to avoid this plague of the Trail by careful personal hygiene, boiling water before drinking it, and taking great care about eating.

With his help we now had a clinic, staffed by a doctor and a registered nurse, both committed Christians who worked like Trojans, night and day, for no pay. It was a miracle!

The clinic drew a steady stream of people whom we confronted with the gospel and led to Christ. God was beginning to put all the pieces together for us, and the establishment of the free clinic was a big, important breakthrough. We could never have planned it, never have hoped to set things up the way that they occurred. But the right people and the right conditions "just happened" to come together at just the right time.

Eight

Surprised by "Joy"

Many travellers who would never have been attracted to us just by the prospect of free tea and conversation came in basically because they were sick enough to seek help anywhere and once they got to us, they stayed.

One of the first of these initially reluctant visitors was Gunther, who was brought to the Olfat with a near-fatal case of typhoid. Travelling illegally without a passport, the young German's mind was burned out by drugs, and he was teetering on the edge of psychosis when he arrived. Richard put him in "isolation" - in a small side room - for a fortnight, so that he could be nursed through the disease without infecting others. He lay in his bunk those two weeks radiating fear continuously; his eyes darted, constantly wide and moving, he believed that we were holding him prisoner, and that our dog was a dragon. He seemed schizophrenic, and was extremely violent when off drugs. Once he jumped out onto the top floor of the building, threatening to commit suicide. He would suddenly take swings at people, muttering vague threats at all who crossed him. At times we had to sedate him to prevent him from hurting himself or others. For a while it seemed that Gunther was going to remain beyond our ability to help.

We were not psychiatrists, but we prayed for God to help us help Gunther, to give us the right instincts and the

right intuitive "therapy" that he required. Gradually,
Gunther began to improve. His violent behaviour
subsided, he began to think more clearly, and was able to
collect his thoughts for increasingly longer periods of
time. He then started to attend our prayer meetings,
attempting to talk to God, and to understand the religious
teaching we represented.

By the winter, Gunther was remarkably better, and at
our Christmas party we gave him a small gift - a vest and
a pair of gloves. He was extremely moved by the gesture -
they were the first Christmas presents he had ever
received in his life! After that Gunther improved rapidly.
He seemed well, and the delusions stopped. Finally, after
spending six months with us, he left to return to Germany
- a different man from when he came to us. He never fully
accepted Christ as his Saviour, which disappointed us all.
But the last I heard he was working steadily as a
carpenter, and I pray that some day, somewhere, he may
meet the Carpenter's Son. One thing is sure - without
God's help in Kabul, he might never have lived for that
opportunity.

Another of the early patients who came to the free
clinic and stayed was Joy, an American Jewish college girl,
who had abandoned her studies in the States to learn in
Jerusalem. But after just a couple of months there she was
less interested in her own Hebrew faith than in the
Eastern religions of which she had heard so much - so she
dropped out again, this time to travel along the Trail to
India.

She never made it. She was bitterly disillusioned by
what she found on the Trail, and she picked up a bad case
of lice - not uncommon in Afghanistan. By the time she
reached Kabul she was in desperate need of medical help,
and arrived at the Olfat after seeing the clinic advertised
on a poster at the little hotel in which she was staying. At
the Olfat she was treated by Richard who, as he so often

did, got into conversation about the Lord, and finished the "consultation" by inviting her back to our living quarters for dinner. She was impressed by the friendliness and openness of the people she met, and intrigued by the sense of peace she felt pervaded the premises. She left with a copy of Francis Schaeffer's book *The God Who Is There* tucked under her arm, and when she brought it back a few days later we invited her to stay with us a week or two and measure the claims of our faith by what she saw among us. A friendship developed between Joy and Sally and they spent a lot of time together. Joy refused to give in easily, though she waited for an outward sign of God's reality. "God, reveal Yourself to me, and I will believe," she would pray fervently in our little prayer room. There seemed to be no answer, and she became increasingly desperate in her sense of need, her prayers more and more passionate and longing.

For Joy, the journey from where she was to where God wanted her to be was a long one. It was an uphill, intellectual struggle for her all the way. She was cynical and tough, much too sceptical of the claims of Christ to be able to assume a posture of faith overnight. She had to overcome all the barriers erected by her anti-Christian background: she was Jewish, she would maintain, and had no need for a Jesus. Working with Joy, we learned the slow lesson of patience and love. We talked, reasoned, taught and prayed with her as she fought her way through the tangle of intellectual and emotional scepticism that kept her from God.

Finally, on Christmas Eve, she discovered the reality of God for herself. With a Finnish friend she went to a special service at the Kabul Christian Community Church, and suddenly, midway through, she began to sob uncontrollably. She cried her way through the rest of the service and on returning to the Olfat declined dinner, going instead straight to the prayer room. Later that night

Sally and I prayed with her, and her heaviness lifted - and a few days later she finally, firmly, fiercely became convinced that Jesus was the Messiah, and claimed Him as her Lord.

Her life definitely changed. The next Sunday she took part in her first communion service, and in the weeks she remained with us her faith blossomed and flowered, even though there were many problems to overcome. Eventually she left Kabul to attend a school of evangelism sponsored by YWAM in Lausanne, and while she was there God continued to confirm His reality to her, through meeting her financial needs in a number of miraculous ways. One time she felt she should go home to visit her parents - since God was guiding her on the visit, Joy felt she should make the arrangements for the trip without worrying about how to pay. In her prayer-time God told her not to worry, as the money would come in the mail on a particular day - and sure enough it did! It was in these kinds of experiences that God was taking extra steps to teach Joy His ways and His character.

Later Joy returned to the States permanently, and having completed the search that had interrupted her studies several years before, went back to campus. Trained as a doctor, today she is married with a young family, and combines the gentle concern for both body and spirit first shown her in a make-do clinic on another Continent. We are still great friends and keep in regular contact.

Manfred was another of the early converts whose surrender to Christ marked the wane of Satan's sabotage attacks. A German "acidhead", Manfred was a psychiatrist's dream - and, for us, briefly a nightmare. He was a walking case study, his head full of a cocktail of quirks and hang-ups. He was greatly troubled by his illegitimacy, guilty about homosexual relationships as a child and plagued by fear of demons and hexes as a result of dabbling in the occult. In short, Manfred was a mess! On one occasion he flung himself headlong down a long flight of stairs in the Olfat, cracking his front teeth and gashing his face in the process.

He had been brought along by a member of our team who had found him alone in a room while touring one of the nearby hotels. For five days after his arrival Manfred was so spaced-out on drugs that he couldn't sleep. At the end of that long period of wakefulness he quietly slipped into the bathroom and slashed his wrists. We found him, blood pulsing from his wrists in dark red splurts, and managed to stop the bleeding just in time. Another time he swallowed a monstrous overdose of tranquilisers, and we had to rush him to the hospital to get his stomach pumped.

When Manfred decided that he'd had enough of us, he departed in spectacularly individual fashion. As we all knelt in prayer during devotions on the sixth floor, he ran out onto the balcony. One of the team went out to bring him back, only to return ashen-faced, wide-eyed - and alone.

"He's gone! He's not out there," he gasped.

Immediately we all rushed out and peered over the edge of the balcony, expecting to see Manfred's body sprawled hideously on the street six floors below. But Manfred had not actually jumped at all. He had leapt over the balcony, swung down onto the one below, then jumped down onto the ground. We were certain that we would never see him again, but later that same evening the door swung open, and there he stood.

"I left my sweater behind," he explained lamely. "And I thought that I had better come back and get it."

It was a pitiful excuse, a flimsy substitute for the real message in Manfred's heart, which was screaming: "I want to come back because I need you to care about me. Please don't stop trying to help me!" So that night he went with us to the prayer room, where we prayed for him till late in the night, rebuking the evil powers in his life. Manfred repented of his sins and immediately went to sleep - he, the insomniac of citywide repute. He came to breakfast the next morning a different person, and was never the manic old Manfred again.

From that time Manfred had a powerful testimony in all the hippy hotels around. With his new life and outlook he went straight out onto the streets again, and he brought many young people back to us over the next few months. Old friends, including some of Jacques' evil circle, came right into the Olfat to try to entice him to shoot up with them again, but he was adamant in his refusal. Finally they left him alone.

Several months later Manfred was strolling along a street in Zurich when he spied a group of young Christians conducting an open air meeting. In the team was a member of our original Kabul team, and Manfred joined him at the microphone in that Swiss street meeting - an unlikely reunion by any standards.

Once the clinic was set up and running reasonably well, and supplied by local doctors, Richard and Jane Winter continued on their way, leaving Jeanette Boteler to run it.

Although Sally had had no medical training, when we worked with YWAM teams all over the world she often did first aid or took care of people until a doctor arrived. At the clinic she learned how to do a lot of practical things to help and, although hesitant at times, she knew her limitations and was not nervous in assisting medically. Many of the hippies suffered from abscesses and Richard taught Sally how to drain them and also how to give certain injections. In some circumstances she said that the only way to cope was to pluck up courage, say a prayer and get on with it!

Walter was a hippy who came in again and again to

have his abscesses seen to and Sally got to know him well. On his last visit to us it was obvious that he was very ill, but he refused to have any treatment. Sally was relieved when someone offered to pay Walter's fare home to Switzerland and hoped that once there, he would be able to get the medical help he needed so desperately. We learnt later, however, that he had died only a few days after his return home and Sally, who had spent so much time caring for him, felt his death deeply.

During those hectic times, God was showing us that despite all, He still had the upper hand - that Satan could not keep from the Saviour those who really seek Him. In Arthur we saw how even the most hard-nosed junkie could be brought to the cross by the gentleness and graciousness of God's Spirit. Twenty-two and from Montreal, Arthur had five long years of heavy drug abuse - hashish, acid and speed. He'd dropped out of school and drifted down to California, where he had been arrested on a drugs charge. After serving time in jail, Arthur slid into a state of depression for two years, living on tranquilisers and sessions with a psychiatrist. Deciding to break away, he hitched his way to the island of Crete and then headed for India, but he never made it.

Stranded in Kabul with no cash, he took a job running a travellers' hotel, and began selling and smuggling drugs. Once he was arrested for dealing in morphine, but managed to buy his way out of jail after a short time. Then two of the team dropped by and invited him over to the chai house. He refused brusquely, but they asked a second and a third time. Arthur was having none of it.

"Listen, guys, I'm a Jew, and I don't want to be converted, OK? So just leave me alone." But they persisted, and eventually Arthur gave in and dropped by.

Once the ice was broken he returned frequently, and God gradually pulled him closer and closer. On one visit, though, his growing warmth towards us evaporated, and he waved a copy of *The Living Proverbs* under my nose, demanding to know why he had been given it to read on his last visit. I didn't know, and was rather surprised myself - it's an unlikely evangelistic tract to give to a Jew! But God used even that awkward situation. Arthur was angry because when he had read it through he had come across many references to sins such as sexual immorality, pride and criticism - which he had underlined - and thought that we were obliquely condemning him. We explained that wasn't the case and that what had happened as he read the book was that God's Holy Spirit had started to bring conviction into his heart about many of those things.

Not long afterwards Arthur gave his heart to Christ in as quiet and sedate a prayer as you ever heard. You would never have known, listening to him talk his way into his Heavenly Father's family that night, that he was an emotionally bruised and wounded young man.

From that time on, Arthur was almost obsessively in love with the Bible. It became the single most important thing in his life, and he carried it everywhere with him, reading it constantly. One day he asked to have a private talk with me. When we went on one side, he silently handed me a list of Bible verses, all of which had to do with love, particularly the concept of brotherly love. I looked down at the neat, carefully written list of Scripture references, and then over at Arthur.

"Do you understand?" he asked gently.

"Yes, I think I do," I answered with an inward smile at the thought of this young man, once so livid that God's Word should expose his inadequacies and selfishness, now using it to tenderly and lovingly confront someone else.

"Well, I forgive you," he told me. It was Arthur's way of telling me that he felt I had been unloving toward him - that somehow I had not treated him as a brother, but that he forgave me for it all the same. I was deeply touched by the simplicity of the moment. Here was the warm, soft way in which a former junkie, drug smuggler and depressive psychotic expressed himself and cared for others now that Jesus had become his Lord.

Nine

Breakthrough

It's fascinating to consider all the different methods that God uses to communicate with His children.

He talked to us in many ways in Kabul - often through His Word, or through the quiet witness of His Spirit, but occasionally in more dramatic ways, too. And when the first few weeks of battling with Satan for supremacy were over, in addition to the obvious signs of an increasing fruitfulness in our work, God chose another inspiring way to tell us that a new day had dawned for our embryonic mission.

The spectacular confirmation that God was honouring our labours came in the third week of October, after we had been in Kabul getting on for two months, and we were beginning to identify and respond to the demonic threat posed by the likes of Jacques, Patsy and their companions.

The occasion was a water baptismal service for those new believers who had never expressed their faith in this way. This was to be the turning point of our work there. The full significance of that brief Sunday afternoon service is only really appreciated against the backdrop of religious life in Afghanistan - one of the few Moslem countries in the world where it was against the law for natives to be Christians, or to make public statements about Jesus. It was a crime literally punishable by death for an Afghan to convert to Christianity. Such drastic measures were not actually taken while we were there, but had been before we arrived and we understand after we left as well. This was the Afghan attitude towards Christianity. Missionaries were not allowed inside the country. The Kabul Christian Community Church was the only Christian church in the entire land, and was tolerated only on the strict understanding that it ministered solely to the diplomatic corps and other Europeans living and working in the city.

Since we were officially described by the embassies as a Red Cross style outpost for the Western travellers, and not as religious propagandists, we were able to persuade the Kabul authorities to let us stay. We were, after all, helping to alleviate some of the overwhelming problems caused by the crush of sick and needy young people stranded over there - and they needed all the help they could get. Even so, we were not exactly welcomed, but rather grudgingly and suspiciously tolerated. As a result, we took great pains to avoid looking or acting like missionaries to onlookers, and we avoided any contact with native Afghans which had even the appearance of witnessing. Despite the restrictions, though, we did manage to strike deep and lasting friendships with some of the Afghan people we came to know during our time in Kabul.

As if to underline the seriousness of the Afghan religious laws, and the dangers of transgressing them, a travelling Swedish minister was arrested in Kabul the very week we arrived. His wife and family were put under house arrest, and he was held for trial. His crime - distributing a dozen copies of the Gospel of Luke to Afghans.

Not even the respected, long-standing ministry of Dr. Christy Wilson was immune from this governmental antagonism. His church building, a beautiful new sanctuary, built for the diplomatic corps, was abruptly and arbitrarily condemned by government officials - and within days Afghan army bulldozers were knocking the structure to the ground as we stood with members of the congregation and watched helplessly. The sad afternoon was punctured with a moment of grim humour, though. When we asked the soldiers why they were searching so hard through the rubble and foundations, we were told they were looking for the underground church!

After this, services were held in a house next door to the site. There did not seem to be any objection to Christians meeting together, it was more to the actual church building. In our home now we still have a piece of marble which I found in the rubble and gave to Sally. She is delighted to have it as a reminder of the church in Kabul.

The Kabul Christian Community Church had been established for twenty years, and its membership comprised mainly staid, middle-class, middle-aged European business people and diplomats from around the world. In the language of the Trail, they were "superstraight" - almost without exception - the very epitome of establishment roles and identities. Dr. Wilson and some of the leaders may have shared a vision for outreach to the rebellious young Westerners who were flooding into Kabul, but to most the idea of flinging wide the church doors to these "dirty, diseased, long-haired layabouts" was a revolutionary and frightening idea. It was a natural reaction, of course. No different from that of almost any church in America or England. The gap between the diplomats and the hippies was wide - morally, culturally and spiritually. When church members were persuaded to attempt to span that chasm, it was with some hesitation and considerable anxiety on both sides. To the straights, the young people were symbols of sin and social irresponsibility.

Conversely the hippies did not exactly foster open-hearted love for their respectable fellow Westerners. They had their doubts and reservations, too, about going to a "straight" church, and sitting on a pew next to the very types of people whom they had rejected long ago as narrow and hypocritical. The sense of estrangement on both sides could not be banished in a day, with a single magic prayer or sermon. Both sides had some soul-searching to do if the two radically different worlds were to be mingled, even in the context of the "unity" of Christian worship.

An early attempt at bridge-building was to put both sets of people together informally and let them get to know each other. After morning service, each of the newly-converted travellers from our growing community went home for lunch with a church family. At first it was a strained and tight affair. In retrospect, it was funny to see the mutual nervousness of the short-haired, middle-aged diplomat and the bearded, bead-wearing hippy walking off side-by-side for a conventional Sunday lunch! All across Kabul that first Sunday the hippies and the straights were tentatively feeling one another out in conversation, trying determinedly to put aside the well-learned prejudices and stereotypes, and to have genuine fellowship with one another as brothers and sisters in the Lord.

Gradually, in the weeks that followed, the doubts and misgivings fell away, and the "straights" of the Kabul church, and the new Christian "freaks" of the Trail learned to be natural and care for one another. They did so because on both sides they were disciples of Jesus Christ. They really did believe in the love of God which binds, heals and makes all men brothers, regardless of their background, social class or views.

It didn't happen overnight, but by that autumn afternoon when we arrived at the shore of Karga Lake for the baptismal service, it was deepening. About twenty-five of us in beads and sandals were met by a crowd of about seventy-five Community Church members in business suits and dresses who had come to join their Christian brothers and sisters in an emphatic testimony to the presence of Jesus Christ in Kabul. We were absolutely thrilled at their act of support. Though we may have seemed an incongruous, even laughable, mix to an outside observer, I'm certain the gathering warmed God's heart.

It hadn't been a sense of history that kept us going as we made our plans for the baptisms, just a feeling that this was a step God wanted us to take. But there turned out to be deep significance in that lakeside declaration of faith.

Almost three years of scorching drought had shrunk the lake to a fraction of its normal size. Instead of a picturesque stretch of water almost three-quarters of a mile across, it was little more than a large muddy fishpond, just a couple of hundred yards wide. The sun beat down as we stood near to the water's edge, on the dried, parched mudbed which had cracked into large pieces like a giant jigsaw puzzle.

As we began the joyful service with chorus singing and the reading of a passage of Scripture, the weather changed dramatically. The intense heat of the high sun was mercifully cut off as large, dark clouds appeared overhead. The temperature dropped almost immediately, refreshing us in the cool breezes. For only three o'clock in the afternoon, it was uncommonly dark and gloomy, and the lake was enveloped in an eerie atmosphere.

The first of the young people to be baptised - Paul from Germany - waded out until the grey water reached up to his waist. As the minister pronounced the blessing, the wind whipped and howled around him. He finished with the words, "In the name of the Father, the Son, and the Holy Spirit," and dipped the young man backwards into the water. As he raised him up again, dripping and smiling, there was another abrupt change in the weather.

Like the Red Sea in the Bible days, the dark clouds began to part, exposing a light blue sky. The wind dropped, the clouds rolled away, and as we turned our faces upwards into the warm sun, it began to rain! Big, heavy drops of water splashed down as the heat rippled over us again.

One of the Community Church members broke the awed silence, turning to me to whisper: "Did you realise that this is the first public baptism to have been held in Afghanistan for over one thousand years?"

It was a fantastic stirring moment. There was a great, surging, release of the Spirit. I felt the power and oppression of Satan himself being broken, and falling in pieces around my feet. All around the edge of the Lake, people began to cry quietly and to praise God. Hippy and straight alike, it made no difference - we all stood enraptured as God's Spirit bathed us.

In that majestic, soaring feeling of victory, we all knew that God was confirming the rightness of our presence in the country by breaking the fierce drought that had gripped Afghanistan for so long.

God had honoured the obedience of His people, and He was now telling us that the oppression of Satan was over, his ground lost. It was a wonderful, emotional moment as we stood there in the sunlight on the edge of the water, praising and thanking God for His message to us. We knew that we had turned the corner once and for all. There, in the hostile and unwelcoming, barren land of Afghanistan, we had testified that in Jesus all men are one and He had signalled that He was with us all the way.

Ten

Open Heart - Open Home

As more and more people were drawn to the Olfat by our popular chai house and free clinic, we felt the pinch in our crowded living quarters on the fifth floor.

Our concept of evangelism had always been one of deliberate, patient presentation of the claims of Jesus. Our strategy was simple - to attract the young people to the place and, if they wanted to live among us and learn more about the Christian life, to invite them to do so. We believed in letting them see for themselves whether or not the gospel we preached really worked in practice. We had seen too much firing-from-the-hip evangelism - the kind in which an earnest Christian slaps someone on the back, peppers him with a canned three-minute speech on the need for repentance and salvation, quotes a well-worn Bible verse or two, and then asks the poor target to bow his head and "let Jesus come in". We had seen too much of it - and so had the travellers - to believe very strongly in its value.

Almost all the folk on the Trail had, at one time or other, been "evangelised" - maybe as a teenager back home, on the college campus, or elsewhere. And, unfortunately, many of those experiences had been bad ones. They lacked any expression of real concern, any depth of love and caring, and the recipients of such attention left those exchanges more resentful of religion than ever.

It was important to remember that the young people were "dropping out" because they hated the coldness and impersonal style of modern life. They felt the tension of their age, and many had been cheated out of intimate relationships even with their parents by the demands of the consumer era. Consequently, they had become alienated, and turned to a culture which was by contrast slow, relaxed and personal in its relationships.

We sensed the resentment these young people would feel if someone walked up to them and tried to squeeze them into their five-steps-to-heaven mould, before waltzing away and onto the next target.

If such "quickie evangelism" was not effective with folk in general - and from what we had experienced there was plenty of evidence to suggest that was the case - then it was especially futile with the sensitive young people we were attempting to reach. These hardened, nomadic renegades weren't going to be attracted to us if we only showed a superficial interest in them. It would take time, love and lots of patience.

We felt that the best way to share Jesus with these young people was simply to make ourselves available to them. Everyone who came through the doors would receive our medical help and food. As we felt led, we shared our love for the Lord with them.

Those who wanted to dig deeper into what we were talking about - by studying the Bible, cross-questioning us about our beliefs, and watching our lives - we would invite to stay for a week or two. When people accepted Christ, we considered it our responsibility to nurture and teach them in the ways of God until they were ready to go on in life as more mature, well-developed followers of Jesus.

This kind of approach, however, took time, space and a relaxed environment. While the Olfat Hotel was perfect for meeting newcomers, it was a terrible setting in which to attempt to take people on further. Visitors were constantly coming and going, and the noise of the city was clearly audible. It was a poor substitute for a quiet, peaceful Christian retreat. Besides which, as it was a hotel, we had no control over access to the top two floors.

Clearly we needed a house with more room - preferably well out of the downtown hippy district. It needed to be big, inexpensive, and close to the bus route into town. After a few months we started looking for such a place. We prayed, squeezed into our little Citroen and began driving up and down the streets looking for a suitable place. We found just what we needed and were surprised and pleased that the rent was nearly half of what we had expected to pay.

The house in question was about four miles from the Olfat area of Kabul, and only two blocks from a bus stop. There were twenty-three rooms in the building, and it had a high stone wall around the yard plus a private well. It was perfect for our purposes. We now had room to house the team, with plenty still left over for guests to join us without over-crowding the place. It was a home for converted hippies to grow in God without the distraction of the Olfat, and a place for Christians to minister to them in a relaxed, easy going atmosphere.

Although we had little money and there was little material available, Sally set out to make our new house into a home. It wasn't easy but she used her creative gifts to make the place inviting with a few simple furnishings.

Our desire was to create an atmosphere of love and peace where our lives as a couple and our unity as a team would touch people with the reality of God's love. We believed that each person God sent to us was a significant individual. God is a personal God: man is not the product of chance, but exists because God made him and longs for a relationship with him.

We therefore sought to include everyone living with us in the responsibility of running the house and making decisions about who came to live with us and how we paid the bills.

We prayed long and hard about a name for the house before settling for "Dilaram House", which means "a peaceful heart" in the Farsi language. In Afghanistan there are thirteen major tribal dialects and Farsi, which is a Persian dialect, is the common trading language. Both Sally and I had soon learnt a few phrases in Farsi, as had many hippies, and we felt the name and interpretation most suitable. We kept the chai house and clinic going back at the Olfat, but now in addition had a refuge to harbour honest seekers who wanted to investigate the Christian life, and those in their early days of life with the Lord.

There were many interesting arrivals that first autumn and winter, among them Paul Sudarkah, a fifty-year old Indian who had spent fourteen years at the feet of a guru in Kerala, India. He travelled one of the strangest routes to Christ I have ever heard. After years of studying in an Indian ashram, he went to southern India's most famous Hindu guru, and implored him: "How can I know the true Krishna, the god of my people?"

The guru's answer was startling. "Go to the book of the Christians, which they call 'The New Testament'. Study the man there named Jesus Christ, and there you will find what you seek. Jesus is the reality and Krishna is but a shadow of that reality."

Strange words indeed. Paul then began to study the Scriptures and soon after committed his life to Jesus. He stayed at Dilaram House for several weeks, giving us invaluable lessons in the history and principles of Hinduism, before going back to India.

Word of our new home spread quickly through the drug community, and with the house being bigger we were able to have more people to stay with us than we had at the Olfat. We thought of ourselves not so much as a team of evangelists anymore, but as a family of Christian brothers and sisters - the Dilaram family, brought together by God, and living in Kabul to provide a witness and a home for the travellers there.

The opportunity to slide between clean sheets at night, to sit at a table with a tablecloth and flowers, to rest among friends with the air free of hashish and profanity, to relax without having to worry about thieves and cut-throats; this was an experience which many of our weary, disillusioned visitors had not enjoyed in many months. For them, just being among us in that sort of setting gave the Holy Spirit all the opening He needed to nudge them back to Jesus Christ. We avoided high-pressure salesmanship tactics, not leaning on the uncommitted for "immediate conversion or else!" We did demand that they obey the house rules - hash and other drugs were forbidden, and everyone was required to help with the daily chores and attend the Bible-study sessions. We did not have a tight, tiring dawn-to-dusk schedule, but we did have a programme, and all who stayed with us were expected to follow it.

Our family at Dilaram House was usually between twenty and forty, but in the summer months when we had short-term visitors it often rose much higher. Sally and I, though young, took on the main "parenting" role in the community, which was a big responsibility. As we were permanent residents, we had our own rooms to which we retreated, but even so it was difficult finding time to be together. As the mother figure, Sally made out rotas for domestic chores and supervised cooking.

At one point nearly everyone in the house went down sick and Sally blamed herself. Food preparation took a long time as all fruit and vegetables had to be peeled and soaked in a special solution and all water, even though it came from a special well, was boiled for twenty minutes. Preparing a single meal for our large family required a huge effort. Sally felt something was wrong with the food preparation but a British doctor in the community put her mind at rest by saying that as Afghanistan was such a disease-ridden place and germs were so prevalent, it was possible to pick up amoeba and bacteria just by breathing in dirty air, especially at certain periods of the year when dust storms blew up nearly every afternoon. Sally was relieved and continued to take the usual food precautions but no longer blamed herself for the sickness.

She worked out a basic menu and Ishmael not only shopped for the food, but used his imagination to produce wonderful meals of an international flavour for us. Rice was the staple diet and as lamb was cheap we had a lot of that and added other meats and different types of vegetables when available.

In Dilaram House we had the time and opportunity to take part in conversations, debates, dialogues and discourses, which were all part of the way of life on the Trail. Some of the most meaningful conversations took place while the household chores were being done and of course meal times were a good opportunity to share ideas and concepts.

Our work seemed to have three basic steps. Firstly, to let the Holy Spirit use our work in the streets and at the Olfat to draw in those who really needed help. Secondly, to commit ourselves to getting to love, know and care for them, making ourselves vulnerable in the process, so that we could help them surrender their lives to God. And thirdly, to keep the new believers with us long enough to ground them in their faith. Making them strong enough to stand the battering they would take on going back to society was vital.

Our method of evangelism was slow and demanding - but for those rebellious young Westerners, it was the only way. Even now, with the dogmatic views of our Afghanistan days tempered with a very real appreciation of the importance of direct, bold evangelism, I believe that treating people with respect is absolutely essential, no matter what approach we use.

At that time our aim at Dilaram House was to give the Holy Spirit the opportunity to reveal Christ through us, as we opened our lives to the world travellers. That meant being vulnerable to them and as a result required a constant effort to stay in God's will and attitude. Getting involved in people's lives in this way is so time consuming, but it is worth every bit of effort. It is easier to say, "Jesus loves you", and move on swiftly, than to say, "Jesus loves you, and I love you too..." because the latter demands that you take time, and demonstrate and live up to that claim.

Christ set the example. When He met sinners on the streets, He followed them home to eat, to visit and get to know them. He listened to their talk of high taxes and rebellious children, sore backs and poor crops, fractious in-laws and all the little workaday problems that make up life. He listened without showing shock or contempt, as they told Him of sins committed, wives betrayed, friends cheated, blasphemy and drunkenness indulged. He was truly a friend of sinners. And then He showed them, in love, the demands and rewards of the Kingdom of God.

For such an unconventional approach, He was Himself called a blasphemer and drunkard, but He persisted in His personal, one-at-a-time, loving style of ministering to people in need.

We began to see with increasing clarity that it was such a style of approach to people which God was blessing and honouring in Kabul, and we keenly bent our backs to the task of making Dilaram House a place where that special kind of love was available to every person God sent our way.

Eleven

A Painful Separation

We were so busy in our work that, almost before we realised it, autumn was fading away and Christmas-time had arrived in Kabul. There is no time of year when the agony of being alone is so intense as during the Christmas season, and even to the young people who had rejected all the greeting-card sentimentality of the society they had left behind, it seemed to bring a special poignancy. Back home were family and friends amid the decorations and carols - but they were a long, long way from home.

We organised a soup party on December twenty-fourth at the chai house, inviting the hippies on Chicken Street to join us for warm broth and companionship. More than a hundred of them squeezed into the Olfat that night, and we thanked God for the contacts we were developing in the travellers' community. We served soup and talked through to the early hours of Christmas morning.

The flow of world travellers through Kabul was seasonal, swelling to human floodtide proportions during the summer, and tapering off late in the autumn before ebbing to a more manageable stream in the winter. It had become clear in the months we had been in Kabul that one house with just eleven workers was woefully inadequate in meeting the great needs with which we were presented. We needed to recruit workers to come to Kabul the following summer and enlist the spiritual support of as many Christians as possible. Our aim was to gather fifty young people prepared to pay their own way to join us in Kabul for a summer outreach. We needed a swarm of young witnesses who were well organised and trained to lead a gentle but determined assault on the hotels in the area.

Equally importantly, we recognised the real need for more prayer backing. I had learnt the value of intercession and that the prayers of "the folks back home" really did make a difference.

One dramatic example of this truth had occurred a couple of years previously, when Sally and I had been working for a time in Africa. Suddenly, in the early hours of the morning Sally had been stricken with bad internal bleeding, and as the minutes ticked away she hovered close to death. Sally was desperately weak, and I was frantically trying to find a doctor to help us when the bleeding stopped as suddenly as it had begun. Sally gradually recovered. Only much later did we discover that Sally's mother, a saintly woman, had been roused from her sleep thousands of miles away at exactly the same time with the distinct impression that God wanted her to pray specifically for Sally's well-being.

The months in Kabul had only confirmed our opinion of the immense value of widely-based spiritual support. We had seen how clearly we were waging war against the forces of darkness as we pitched Christ's flag in their territory, and by the New Year we were emotionally and spiritually exhausted. In addition, the demands of adapting to such primitive living conditions were wearing down our reserves.

To meet our twin needs for spiritual supporters and short-term workers, we arranged that I would leave on a two-month speaking tour of churches and Christian colleges in Europe and America. Even here God showed us His love and faithfulness. With just a week before departure, and the tickets booked, we still only had a few dollars towards the cost of the flights. Then, just three days before take-off, I received a note from someone in the States. It contained a spontaneous, unexpected gift that paid the fare almost exactly.

It was particularly hard leaving Sally in Kabul at this time because it had just been confirmed that she was pregnant. We shared the news with the family in the house and many of them were surprised to realise we were so happy at the idea of becoming parents. On the Trail pregnancies were a great inconvenience and many crude abortions were performed, resulting in a great deal of pain and suffering.

It had never been envisaged that Sally would go to the States with me because the Dilaram Community had only been going a few months. Even if money had been available for her to travel with me, we knew it was right for Sally to stay. She was the only person responsible and mature enough to lead our new ministry. Knowing about the pregnancy made it very hard to be separated at that time, though.

After our three-day honeymoon we had been almost constantly on the go, travelling to over twenty-five different countries in five years to fulfil busy, demanding schedules, and never returning home for very long.

During that time we had travelled to the West Indies and visited about fifteen of the beautiful islands on summer outreaches. Then we went on a round the world tour with a team of eleven people, visiting Hong Kong, Indonesia, Thailand, Singapore, Sri Lanka, India and many countries in Africa, mainly with the purpose of evangelism and starting new fellowships of believers amongst unreached people's groups. It was a very exciting time and we learnt a great deal about different customs, cultures and people during that time.

Despite all the privations and pressures, our nomadic

life together had one blessing - we'd never been apart for any great length of time. Neither of us relished the idea of the long separation but felt it was all part of the Lord's plan for our lives.

Living in a house with up to twenty-five others, some of whom were particularly demanding, is a potential strain on any married couple, even more so if they are responsible for the leadership of the place. In our case, I was guilty in those early months of being too preoccupied with the needs of the Dilaram family, and not mindful enough of Sally's right to, and need for, times of unshared, private married life. We needed to have more time alone, just to share as a couple - and with the wisdom of hindsight I can see that I had not been sensitive enough to that need. It has proved to be a lesson that needs learning again from time to time.

I hadn't realised that a problem existed until the day before I was due to leave on my tour. As it would be our last day together for some time, I had made plans for the Dilaram family to go on an outing.

"Oh Floyd, I'd hoped we could spend the day together. Just the two of us." Sally looked imploringly at me.

"We can't just walk away from the others here, Sally. We have a responsibility, we had to put them first," I replied, not really understanding what she was saying.

"But we don't see each other much - there never seems time to talk."

"Well we work together all day long."

"That's not what I mean," Sally said.

"Anyway, it's arranged now - the day out. Don't look so sad, you know this is the work the Lord has given us to do and there are times when we have to make sacrifices."

Sally began to cry, and after some moments of discussion, we agreed to have part of the day to ourselves, but I still didn't fully realise how insensitive I was being to Sally and her needs.

She came to see me off at the airport the next day. I started my recruiting trip by going to Finland where a Lutheran church had arranged for me to take meetings all over the country. I then flew to Sweden where I thought the same arrangements would have been made. Unfortunately, the correspondence had obviously gone astray in the post and when this wild-looking man from Afghanistan arrived at the airport there was no-one to meet him! I contacted someone whose name had been given to me by a member of the United Nations in Kabul, and he arranged a full itinerary. Through this contact he and I became good friends and often laughed at the memory of our first meeting! From Sweden I flew to the States and was particularly impressed by the interest shown at Wheaton College which resulted in many students coming to help us in Kabul.

When I arrived in Europe, I really began to assess all the changes God had been taking Sally and me through as we adapted to the needs in Kabul. In the busy day-to-day caring of Dilaram and the Olfat there wasn't time to consider the principles that were involved; we just reacted and responded in the way we sensed God was leading. From a distance I began to see the enormous demands such work placed on individuals, couples and families.

The changes which had taken place almost without my noticing were well illustrated when my parents met me in the States. It was almost two years since we had last been together, but there was no traditional reunion.

Seeing my shoulder-length hair, beard and hippy-style clothes, my mom's jaw dropped and she gasped: "Oh my son!" Dad, maybe more immediately conscious that his formerly strait-laced offspring was due to be speaking at his church, looked at me with great dismay and exclaimed: "Oh my God!"

As I travelled from church to church that winter recruiting people and prayer partners, God began to call me to account about my priorities in dividing my time at the Dilaram House. The normal loneliness of separation and the knowledge that Sally was newly pregnant and facing a long winter with the burden of the work on her shoulders were probably part of the reason that my thoughts returned so often to the considerable implications of the kind of life we had chosen. It was proving hard enough to fulfil the work we believed God had called us to as a couple: how would we be able to cope with having a young family, with all the extra pressures and responsibilities that would place on us?

God used that period of separation to teach me some valuable lessons about proper priorities of family life; truths that were to be important anchors in the time to come. When I eventually returned to Kabul after three and a half months, I had a clearer view, and a determination to apply myself to the understanding I had gained about the priorities I believe God intends us to establish and hold on to.

First and foremost we must nurture our relationship with God: that is the first priority for all Christians. It doesn't mean blithely continuing your devotions while the house is burning down and the rest of the family is in uproar, but it does mean that this precious, cornerstone relationship must be maintained, or everything else is less effective.

Next comes family relationships - both with the natural family and the wider "family" of believers. I had been brought up to believe that putting God first automatically meant putting His work first as well. I now realised that these priorities were wrong - it should be God first, then our families and after that God's work.

A good stable marriage with a quality relationship can take outside pressures but if marriage partners don't spend time with one another and give each other priority, then it undermines the marriage commitment. This often results in unnecessary divorces which crush and hurt many people.

Thirdly is our responsibility to non-Christians. However intense our desire, however noble our aspiration to see others come to know Jesus as their Saviour, these relationships must come afterwards.

The reason for this order is that out of the richness of one's relationships at each level flows the emotional and spiritual energy for the next. As we develop a closeness with God, so the capacity for meaningful relationships with our family and Christian brothers develops. As these bonds are enriched, they in turn provide the strength and inspiration to reach the lost, and to share spiritually and emotionally with them. The key is that the levels must be addressed in proper order. Too many times we become so obsessed with doing God's work that we neglect our relationship with Him or we are so busy trying to communicate God's love to sinners or to the work we do for God that we neglect our own families - and communicate unconcern, and a lack of love, to them.

I once heard someone paraphrase the well-known passage from Matthew chapter sixteen: "What good will it be for a man if he gains the whole world, yet forfeits his own family?" That thought troubled me through our winter apart. What good was it if I saw every hippy in Kabul saved, and yet did not share my life with the wonderful wife that God had given me?

I saw clearly that I needed to get my priorities right. I had to be more sensitive to the needs of my wife - and, in due course, my children. I was angry with myself when I recognised how seriously I had underestimated the depths of Sally's agony those first few months in Kabul. I had been so caught up with the demands of the work that I hadn't stopped to consider how she was coping with the transition we were making in our thinking and life-styles. I had simply urged her to "keep a stiff upper lip", when I should have been much more understanding of her feelings and viewpoint. I had developed a habit of exhorting her to be more dedicated to the work and to find her security in the Lord and not in me. I hadn't realised that it was my disobedience to Biblical principles which caused Sally so much pain and insecurity.

Meanwhile, the Dilaram family back in Kabul was in the grip of one of the worst winters in the city's history. Snow had started falling the day after I left in mid-January - and was still on the ground until just before my return in April. Temperatures dropped to forty below zero, sometimes staying that low for days at a time. In all there were nineteen blizzards, all the pipes froze in the house, and it was impossible to thaw them. Water had to be drawn from the well by hand, then carried into the house and heated upstairs for cooking and bathing. There were wood-burning stoves in all the rooms, but the bitter cold caused the fuel supply to run out early in the winter season, and it was possible to keep only one room warm, with a very small primitive electric heater and a small stove. Multiple layers of clothing was the only answer. It became obvious that tales of wolves coming down from the mountains to the city were not just myths. That winter packs of wolves roamed the streets of Kabul after dark, hungrily searching for something to eat. All through the night Sally and the others could hear them howling outside. A little Afghan girl was killed only two blocks away one night and people were warned not to go out without a gun after dark.

Thousands of travellers couldn't leave Kabul because of the weather, as the bitter cold slowed traffic through the Khyber Pass and across the desert to a virtual standstill. It was estimated that two thousand junkies, plus many other youthful travellers, were stranded in the city that February alone, and the conditions certainly exacted a terrible price from them. There were twenty-four deaths by overdose during those freezing weeks, all of them in tacky rooms along Chicken Street. So the Dilaram family was kept busy working in the hotels, conducting Bible studies, and keeping the house running. Fifteen young people stayed at Dilaram throughout the winter, with dozens more coming and going for brief periods.

For Sally it was a time of great trial. Adjusting to the early stages of pregnancy, separated from me for the longest time ever, she also had to accept ultimate responsibility for keeping the work moving ahead. It was a daunting task, and she found herself repeatedly having to cry to God for help.

When I left Sally became the authority figure, and some of the Kabul kids took advantage of my absence to give her a hard time about her middle-class appearance and values. She won the battle by finding her own identity that winter, and in the struggle developed a new insight into her own feelings and attitudes.

"It was wonderful the way the Spirit helped me," she told me on my return. "He helped me go right back into my childhood and realise the significance of things I had forgotten; helping me to understand myself in ways that I never did before; to see why I was the way I was. He showed me how I could adjust to the ministry and still be true to myself. It wasn't necessary for me to play a role for anyone; I could just be me, and He would use me that way."

Throughout the arduous winter Sally and the other Dilaram workers were sustained by the assurance that God was looking after them. He met their financial needs in a series of small miracles week by week. Once the food supply was depleted and the family ate the last of the food for dinner. The next morning, unexpected and unannounced, a friend from the Kabul Christian Community church dropped by with a gift of money -

enough to stock the larders for a few weeks. On another occasion they sat down to eat the last food in the house only to discover later that a married couple among the guests for dinner had tucked a generous amount of money under their plates when they left as a token of thanks.

Sally had to cope with many different kinds of people dropping into the community that winter as well, some who had serious psychological illnesses and others whose minds had been damaged by drugs or influenced by eastern religions. She had no-one to turn to but the Lord and she learnt a new level of dependence on Him. She told me, "It was wonderful, Floyd, to see God working through me - not just through you."

The community fought a spiritual battle all winter and just turned the corner before my return. During the first few weeks of my absence Sally and the team concentrated on just surviving, but by the time I returned they were experiencing real victory. Spiritually, God worked through them to reach more and more travellers. Among those who gave their lives to Christ through those winter weeks were a number of German travellers who later became full-time workers with us. Sally said it was as if the Lord said, "You have won the battle, you passed the test, this is what you were fighting for."

Paul Filidis, who now serves with us in Amsterdam, was one of those German travellers who came face to face with the Lord.

"I was sitting at a table in Sigi's," he remembered, "when three 'Jesus People' came in. I always enjoyed discussing spiritual things, so I talked with them for a long time that night. They told me of their experiences with Jesus Christ, and I told them 'That may be good for you, but I'm going to go to India, find a tree, sit under it and meditate for years - if that's what it takes - until I find the truth.' They invited me along to Dilaram House, so I decided to go."

Paul went to the house that week, and eventually accompanied the folk there to services at the Community Church. On his second visit, an older English lady stopped him in the sanctuary after the service and spelled out the gospel message in no-nonsense terms. He listened to her tell of the love of Jesus, thought about the love and acceptance he had witnessed at Dilaram, and suddenly, unaccountably, began to cry. "It dawned on me that night," he said later, "how helpless and stupid I was, how small and weak in the face of the enormity of the universe and how foolish it was for me to try to find the truth by myself."

During my absence Sally and I had spoken to each other over the phone a few times but most of our contact had been through letters. I knew how hard their life had been in Kabul and I was concerned for Sally in particular knowing her responsibilities.

When I eventually returned, Sally and I had a few days away together.

"Sally, I want you to forgive me," I said.

"What for?" Sally asked, looking puzzled.

"While I've been away, the Lord has shown me lots of things about priorities in my life. I was being idealistic and thought I needed to put God and His work before you. I realise now that's not right."

We looked at each other and Sally's eyes moistened.

"I want to make it up to you. I believe that the Lord will use us together as a family in the future." She forgave me and we prayed together. I didn't realise then how prophetic those words would turn out to be.

Twelve

My First Time in Jail

I'll never forget the first time I entered an Afghan jail. It was an experience that rocked me back on my heels as hard as the day I strolled into the courtyard at the Bandamir and came face to face with the realities of life as a junkie.

It was an old, decrepit place called Firehouse Prison - so named because it shared a building with a garageful of fire trucks. Located just off Chicken Street, the Firehouse Prison was used for foreigners, mostly hippies who had been arrested on drug charges.

For some unknown reason, the prison authorities were kindly disposed towards us and on this particular day they let us in with no hassle. I walked through the gate into the dark, musty prison, squinting to see after coming in from the bright sunlight. There was a long courtyard with rough walls, and cells down both sides. They were just fifteen paces by twenty, and had up to a dozen people in each with nothing but a few tattered char-pais on the mud floors.

In the first cell were two British and two American long-haired drop-outs. Each of them had been in prison for more than a week, and had not yet seen a judge, lawyer or embassy official. As we walked further, rats scurried across the floor and huge insects scuttled everywhere. Typhoid, dysentery and hepatitis victims were mixed in with the healthy prisoners. Some of the young prisoners were bruised and battered, reminding us of the tales that in the Firehouse Prison a scruffy Westerner could expect to be beaten at the lightest provocation.

We met a Jewish kid named Arnold, who was in for smuggling. We met a red-haired lad, young and scared, who was suffering from morphine withdrawal, doubled over in pain. Then there was Eddie, who had knifed an Afghan in a vicious fight. We also met a hippy whose girlfriend had been arrested at the same time....but she had bought her freedom by sleeping with the guards. He was shattered, and despaired of ever seeing the outside again. My first impression of the jail stayed with me and no matter how many times I visited, the squalor and suffering inside those dingy cells appalled me. The conditions in which people were meant to live were atrocious.

When we prayed for God to send desperately-needed married couples to help our work at Dilaram, we had no idea that we would find the answer to that petition in a Kabul prison. Their names were Ron and Jan, and they were in many ways typical of thousands of other American couples on the road. They had dropped out of their middle-class Californian life and headed for the East independently, their paths crossing in Greece. Hitching their way along the Trail together, by the time they reached India their bodies were run-down. In Bombay they were introduced to opium dens, and mere smoking was soon not good enough for Jan; she actually ate opium one night and was made violently sick. When she had partially recovered, they travelled on to Goa, where Ron developed hepatitis. They then decided they must get home to America as soon as they could travel back across the Trail.

When they got back to the States, Ron and Jan were

married in a small, private ceremony and rented an apartment in California. But their aversion to the American way of life was still there. The old restlessness, the thirst to travel, had never fully been shaken, and they began to think about striking out on the Trail once again. Some weeks later a friend of Ron's sold him a large amount of LSD - that was all the excuse they needed to pack up and head East. They smuggled the psychedelic drug into Europe and sold it to American servicemen in Germany and other hippies in Greece, making nearly one thousand dollars a month. With this they headed for Kabul where they bought a supply of hashish, hid it in the false bottom of an accordian case, and booked a flight back to Europe.

Friends had warned them that smuggling overland was much safer than by air, but the couple ignored the advice. They figured that their stash was pretty well hidden, and the profit waiting in Europe would make it worth the risk. They were searched at Kabul airport and the hashish discovered. After an exhausting day of answering police questions, they were booked and thrown into separate cells. For the first time, they were scared.

As Ron was being hauled into a police car for the trip to Central Prison, he saw a group of hippies walking past and yelled at them to get word to the United States embassy that he was being jailed. A little while later he was pushed into the prison's main open cell. It had a filthy dirt floor and adobe walls; dozens of prisoners lay around on the ground and on a few char-pais. There were no toilets, only three holes in the middle of the ground, side by side. The prisoners had more drugs than food, and fights broke out frequently.

Ron was then hustled along to the captain's office, where the guards shook whips in his face, yelled Farsi, which he didn't understand, at him and jerked him around the room by his long ponytail. Then they threw him into a locked cell alone. During that time Ron finally began to think seriously about himself, questioning his reasons for the life he had chosen. After two days he was let out of solitary confinement and returned to the open cell with other prisoners. He was surprised at how free he felt just to be out of the small, closed cell.

In the meantime, Jan had been kept in prison also but as a result of the intervention of Jim Murray - an official at the American embassy with whom we had a good relationship - she was released after two weeks on the understanding that she came to us at Dilaram House. Jan made a deep, genuine commitment to God at the Community Church one night and she immediately began praying for God to help her husband.

At the Central Prison, Ron was allowed one visitor for an hour each Saturday. On the first Saturday after her release, Jan - by now already a Christian - went to see him. He rushed eagerly to the visiting area to meet her, but was stunned by what she had to say to him.

"Ron, I've met the Lord. I'm a Christian now and I'm staying at a Jesus house, and we're all praying that God will help you get out of here."

He couldn't believe what he was hearing! Was this really Jan, his travelling-partner-turned-wife, his companion in opium and hash and speed, his accomplice in smuggling - was this his hippy wife, Jan? Ron returned to his spot on the prison floor more bitter than ever before in his life. He felt betrayed and double-crossed by her. He sat rotting in a scummy jail, and his wife had lost her mind and joined up with the Jesus people!

But Jan returned to YWAM house to wrestle with God for her husband's soul, and God gave her the assurance that he would come through. She kept returning to the Central Prison each week, taking Ron small gifts, and telling him confidently that God was going to work things out. Then after ten weeks, Ron was suddenly and inexplicably released. With nowhere to go, he joined Jan at Dilaram. While there, he set up another drug deal, this time smuggling hash oil - a concentrated liquid form of the cannabis plant from which hashish is made - to the States. Somehow, though, when the time came to finalise the deal, Ron pulled back. He returned to Dilaram House, and a few days later give his life to Christ, too.

Ron and Jan were changed people. They wrote to their parents, asking for forgiveness for all the tears and turmoil they had caused. They stayed with us for nine months in Kabul, growing steadily in their faith, and later spent several years with us as full-time workers in Amsterdam before eventually returning to the States to pick up their studies. But this time the aimless wanderlust was gone, replaced with a purpose and a goal - Jesus was in their lives.

If a Kabul jail was an unlikely source for the married couples we were seeking so keenly to join our work, then so, too, were the tacky hotel rooms dotted all over the downtown district - which is where we found Peter and Kate Fitzgerald.

Travelling overland to Australia from Europe, their marriage was in a really bad way by the time they reached Afghanistan and Peter's health was even worse, but his sickness had kept them together. He lay desperately ill in their cheap hotel room while Kate, who was not well herself, went off to try and find help. We found them on one of our regular tours and brought them back to the house, where we nursed them both back to health. As they recovered they began to examine our Christian claims, and it wasn't long before Kate asked God to come into her life.

For Peter it was to be a much longer, lonelier search. It was his isolation and urge to get away from people that had brought them to Kabul in the first place. From the island state of Tasmania, the couple had gone to London because Peter wanted to escape from people, and where better to find an anonymous uninvolved existence, he figured, than in a vast metropolis like England's capital city? But even loneliness in a crowd wasn't enough, and after a few years they decided to return "down under", with the dream of escaping totally from civilisation and living in a lighthouse off the coast of Australia. They were on their way to India to catch a boat when sickness brought them to us in Kabul.

While Kate grew slowly in her newfound faith, Peter fought hard against it but finally he came, reluctantly, to the point where he was convinced intellectually that Christianity's claims were true - but then he despaired.

"I looked inside myself, and I saw that I didn't want the truth!" he told me in anguish. "It made me wonder what kind of person I was if I believed that something was true, and didn't have the moral integrity to choose it or want it!"

In his disappointment and disbelief at his own emptiness Peter even considered suicide - something which, to me at least, demonstrated that he was a man of real integrity. Then, through another bout of sickness, Peter was treated by a gentle, caring man, Dr. Herb Friesen, who impressed him greatly with his concern and compassion. Finally, Peter accepted Jesus as his Saviour.

It was a decision without emotion, but Peter professed to me: "I've come to believe that Jesus is the truth, so I'll serve Him even if I never feel anything about it for the rest of my life." And for a few months he did just that, with no intimate experience or emotions. Just a bare bones commitment to what he had come to recognise as the truth. And then, lovingly, God responded to Peter's integrity and honesty with a tender, warming touch of His Spirit.

After a few months with us, Peter and Kate moved on to a similar house that had been set up by some of our workers in Nepal, where despite their spiritual youth they provided valuable help to the leadership. When I visited them as they prepared to return to Australia, I asked them to consider returning to Nepal to lead the Dilaram work there on a long term basis. They agreed but once back in Australia, they were unable to find a church where they felt accepted and comfortable. Gradually their commitment to Christ waned, until the flame seemed to have died out.

When a Salvation Army officer they had met on the boat home contacted them by 'phone, they wanted nothing more to do with Christians. Kate pretended that the man had the wrong number, but he wasn't to be deterred. He called again a couple of weeks later asking to speak to the Fitzgeralds.

"Sorry, there's no-one here of that name. You must have the wrong number," Kate replied.

Still he wouldn't leave it there. When the determined Salvationist telephoned for a third time a few days later, they finally admitted who they were, and confessed what had happened to their love for God. Their new friend came to see them, and the three of them prayed together for forgiveness and a restoring of Peter and Kate's relationship with their Heavenly Father. They then recommitted their lives to Christ.

Even when he talks about it today Peter cannot help but pause, sometimes with tears in his eyes, as he gives a double testimony to God's love - explaining how when God makes a covenant He never goes back on His pledge, but pursues us with faithfulness and compassion.

After their brief estrangement from God, Peter and Kate settled down into fellowship at an Australian church where they were adopted as missionaries before returning to take over the leadership of the house in Nepal. They spent two years there before we invited them to join us in the work we had by that time begun in Amsterdam.

During their time in Holland they led one of the busiest aspects of our work for five years, a Dilaram-style ministry through which over one hundred people a year came to Christ.

Some of their heart was still out in the East, though. In 1980 Peter and Kate moved to New Delhi, where they started a work among the urban poor Indians - the poorest of the poor, living in feeble shanties and scraping a living from day to day. They established a supplementary feeding programme, a literacy scheme and an out-patient clinic, before returning to Australia recently for the educational needs of their own four children.

To junkies and Third World slum dwellers, Peter and Kate reached out their caring hands in the name of Christ time and again, always prepared to get involved, come alongside, love and serve. What a remarkable transformation for the couple who were once running away from everyone!

Thirteen

How to Sleep through a Revolution

We had been given a beautiful boxer dog whom we called Smack, who became a part of the Dilaram family and was a friend to everyone.

When Sally was first pregnant she was so sick that she lost a great deal of weight and was prescribed anti-nausea tablets. Smack was a very excitable dog, and one day he ate some of the tablets, which made him hallucinate and go "on a trip" which was both funny and sad to watch, but he soon recovered.

We were later given a small dachshund by a diplomat returning home to Germany. Herbie and Smack did not get on very well together but were a great source of amusement to many of the hippies. The presence of these dogs contributed to our family atmosphere, as would our new baby due later in the summer.

Having a baby in our circumstances was not going to be easy and we both had to sort a lot of things out with the Lord about the wisdom of raising a family in Kabul. Being away from our families and knowing that the medical care was not the same as in the West did concern us but we knew the Lord had called us to Kabul and felt that He had said it was time for us to have a family, therefore we trusted that He would take care of both Sally and the baby.

Many members of the Dilaram community had not experienced love or seen a married couple who loved each other and were looking forward to the arrival of a baby in the way we did. Often they were from broken homes and they or their friends had had abortions because a baby would have hindered their lifestyle. As the pregnancy became more noticeable, the hippies asked for progress reports and showed a great interest. Early on they had decided the baby would be a boy so from then on he was affectionately referred to as Moses.

Sally and I lived in a separate section of the house. This was on the second floor at the back where it stuck out above the garden. There was a porch below and on the night "Moses" was due to be born some members of our community stayed on the porch so that they would be amongst the first to know of his arrival. Dr. Jock Anderson, and midwife Pauline Short, delivered Sally at 5.00 in the morning and we were thankful that there were no complications. When Misha let out her first cry a loud cheer went up from the porch and as soon as everything was tidy we wanted them to see our new little girl. Several were a bit disappointed we had a girl rather than a boy because they so liked the name Moses! Even though Sally had been in labour many hours and was tired, we wanted to share our joy and it was a wonderful sight to see long-haired hippies reaching out and touching Misha. It was a very special time. At first the hippies didn't want to hold her because she seemed so small and fragile but, as they got used to her, they cared for her and she became a focal point of the family. The Afghan cook Ishmael, in particular, had a close relationship with Misha and she spent many hours sitting on his knee. He gave his time to her and although he had a family of boys of his own, Misha was special to him.

Misha wore simple Afghan style baby clothes and

sometimes western clothes were brought out to us. The United States Embassy had a Thrift Shop where second hand baby items were sold, and a friend of ours picked up several useful things that way which obviously helped a lot.

Because of their constant travels, many of the young people we worked with were a very dirty group. Some hadn't washed or bathed for months and their clothes were filthy. When Misha got to the crawling stage, at times Sally found she was on the verge of panicking when Misha picked up dirty things and put them in her mouth or touched the face of the hippy holding her. The Lord told Sally that He loved Misha more than she did. Sally learnt a great lesson - she was to do her part in taking the right precautions but in the things she could not control she needed to relax and trust God. Getting this clear in her own mind lifted a large weight of responsibility from her shoulders. It wasn't always easy though and at one point Misha was seriously ill with bacillary dysentery. Even in that situation, however, we both had a wonderful sense that the Lord was in control and we felt a deep peace.

Misha was a lively little girl and being surrounded by so many people stimulated her a great deal. Belonging to a community as we did, we shared her with the family, but she was still our daughter. At times, it was difficult to teach her discipline when others didn't react in the same way as we did. Eventually, we realised we had to clarify what we were trying to do. An ordinary couple with their first child in their own home would not have this problem, but we found we had to ask the Dilaram family to support us so that we all taught the same thing to Misha. It was difficult to do this over such a personal family matter, but we learnt to be more open in our lives. If we were going to share our children, we also needed to be honest in explaining our feelings to the larger family.

At about three o'clock in the morning of July 15th, 1973 when Misha was nearly a year old, we were asleep at Dilaram House when Sally and I were awakened by a popping sound, like muffled firecrackers, outside the walls.

"Floyd, I think that was gunfire!"

"You're crazy," I mumbled, still half-asleep.

"But, Floyd, wake up and listen! Doesn't that sound like machine guns to you?"

"Go back to sleep, Sally," I begged. "It must be noise from that factory down the street."

"Floyd, are you sure? I'm almost positive there's some shooting going on out there!"

"Umhm. You're hearing things. Go to sleep." And with that drowsy response, I followed my own advice and dozed off.

Sally's basic sanity was confirmed two hours later, when all the sounds of a grade-B war movie broke out in ear-splitting profusion over our heads. Squadrons of MiG-21s, Russian-built fighter planes, shrieked by in low passes over the city. The sound of machine gun fire, unmistakable now, broke out in this and that direction. People up and down our road poured from their houses to look up into the sky and scan the street for signs of action.

Afghanistan was having a revolution.

The coup was well planned and perfectly executed. While the king was out of the country, a group of young military leaders moved to depose him and his prime minister, and to install a man of their choice as head of the government. With control of virtually the entire army, they faced little opposition, and by breakfast-time that morning the revolutionary take-over was an accomplished fact. For a few days we lived with a highly visible military control in the city, but with few exceptions the coup was completed without fighting.

The change of government had an almost immediate impact on the world travellers in Kabul. The new military leadership was a stern, no-nonsense corps of army officers, and they had no time for long-haired drop-outs from the West. The new prime minister announced immediately that tourist visas would no longer be granted to hippies or drug addicts, that people trying to enter the country wearing hippy-style dress and long hair would be "discouraged" from so doing, and that a major effort would begin soon to rid the city of its status as a haven for world travellers.

Kabul might remain a major stop on the Trail, but it would no longer be the resting place for down-and-out junkies, or a Nirvana where drugs were cheap and easy to come by. The new government was going to get tough with the world travellers, and the hippy population of Kabul was going to shrink to a mere fraction of its present size.

Before even the first week was over, we saw the seriousness of the new official posture. Every morning after the coup, the police came to the door of Dilaram House to check the passports and visas of everyone there. I had to bring every passport in the house to them, and give a guarantee that none of the members of our community were in violation of the visa laws.

The revolution and its subsequent impact on the hippy community seemed to confirm to us the wisdom of a course we had begun to explore the previous autumn. That was the idea of extending the Dilaram work to other stops along the Trail, all the way from Europe to southern India, as well as in other countries. As more and more of our converts had turned to full-time outreach to other world travellers, and as increasing support and interest from back home made such an ambitious programme possible, the idea of splitting up the Dilaram work emerged. It seemed to be the only alternative to developing a larger and larger staff at Kabul, which we didn't want. We wanted to maintain family-sized units.

The dramatic change in the climate for young Westerners in Kabul underlined our thinking and the wisdom of extending the Dilaram House principle. Our second house had been established a few months previously in Katmandu, the beautiful, lush city in Nepal, set in a valley among the high Himalayas. The storied Shangri-La of literature, Nepal was a thriving centre of Tibetan Buddhism, and a popular final destination for Eastern religion devotees and heavy drug users. The YWAM team began to gain converts among the young people as soon as they had established the base. Its work still continues successfully today - the last Dilaram House in the East still functioning, and this despite the difficulties of working in a country where evangelism of the Nepalis is a criminal offence.

Similar homes were to be opened and run in London and New Delhi for several years, each seeing many travellers and drop-outs come to Christ.

In addition to these points on the Trail, I felt that it was vital for us to have somewhere in Europe acting as a halfway house between East and West. We had seen the difficulties that our converts had in adjusting immediately from life on the Trail to the conventional lifestyle of Western society. We needed somewhere to send them, away from central Asia, where they could take time to get on their feet spiritually, and readjust to the kind of lives they would lead back home.

We also needed a crossover point for the reverse process - for the sincere young Christians in "straight" life back in America and Europe who were willing to help in the outreach along the Trail. Our experience with summer volunteers in Kabul taught us that many were quite unable to cope with the sudden cultural decompression involved in flying straight into an environment like

Chicken Street. They needed to be trained and prepared to make them fully effective when they arrived.

As we looked West, one city seemed to stand out above all the others like a huge landmark - Amsterdam. The centre of the hippy life in Europe, and the fountainhead of the Trail, eastwards, it was spoken of affectionately by many of the world travellers which whom we made contact. They praised its liberal attitudes to drugs and sex and its general sympathy to hippies and drop-outs. From others we talked with, it became clear that this Dutch city was also well-known as a rallying point for devotees of Eastern religions. It seemed that everything with which we were involved was to be found in Amsterdam - a city of the West with a feel of the East.

In fact I had not been able to get the city of Amsterdam out of my mind since I had started praying for it several months earlier. I had the growing feeling that somehow our future destiny was linked to the well-known Dutch city.

Fourteen

Learning the Hard Way

Increasingly, our hearts and thoughts were turning to Amsterdam. Even in the midst of our busy Kabul work, we began to pray weekly for the Dutch city. We also sent one of our workers, Paul Miller, to "spy out the land". The six weeks he spent there fired him with enthusiasm for the potential of a vital work and witness in the city, and his report on returning to Kabul heightened our determination to explore whether we should establish our "bridgehead" ministry there.

Little did we know as we looked toward Amsterdam that we were not the only people who had been drawn to the city. I received a letter from Don Stephens, at that time the European Director of YWAM. The previous year Don had been heavily involved in a massive European evangelism campaign centred around the Olympic Games in Munich. Now he wrote to tell me that he was leading a team for a summer outreach in Amsterdam to work among the swollen population of young tourists and world travellers.

Accommodation for the volunteers was vital, and arrangements had been made for them to use the Salvation Army building right in the centre of Amsterdam. Unfortunately two weeks before they were due to move in, squatters broke into the building. Dutch friends then told Don about two houseboats in the north of the country which had been used as a boarding school for children. They were both over one hundred and fifty feet long with two stories and seemed ideal for his purpose. The only snag was that they were going for 80,000 guilders - and Don didn't have any money!

Undeterred, he prayed about the situation, and felt that God was telling him to offer half the original asking price. He did so - and was delighted when it was accepted. Some Dutch friends helped out with some financing, and soon the two boats had been towed from their berth at Groningen, in the north of the country, lashed together and moored in Amsterdam's main harbour, right behind the central railway station.

When the summer mission was half over, Don wondered what to do long term with the two boats. He felt the Lord prompting him to write to us asking whether we would like to take them over for a new work in the city. Sally and I were excited by this unexpected offer, especially as we had been praying so much for the city. But we felt that despite our growing burden for Amsterdam we still needed clearer guidance from God about whether He wanted us to make this move. We prayed about it and during our team time together read the book of First Chronicles. As we did so we were all deeply moved when we came to the passage which describes how David turned over the building of the Temple to his son, Solomon.

When we had first made what we believed to be a "brief" stopover call at Kabul, God had made it clear that He wanted us to stay and launch a work there by pointing us to a passage of Scripture that spoke about building a temple for Him. Now we sensed that He was showing us He had a new work for us. It was not to be a majestic sanctuary, but a ministry to be founded on the two Amsterdam houseboats.

With great anticipation, we accepted Don's offer. Only

later did we learn that he had been prompted to offer the houseboats to us in the first place after reading in his daily quiet time *that same passage in I Chronicles!*

As the dust settled on Afghanistan's revolution, we prepared for future changes and looked forward to implementing the many lessons we had learnt in our two and a half years in Kabul.

We had learned to give content in our witnessing. Many of us had grown up with religious experience placed ahead of theological content in our list of priorities for telling others about Christ. But we found that, especially for people heavily into Eastern mysticism, religious experience was not a suitable basis for a new faith. The gospel we preached had to be presented with intellectual integrity and historical reality.

Those who were into Eastern religions could offer very reasonable explanations of Hinduism as a system of thought and could shake lots of young, inexperienced Christians with their logic. But the Hindu logic is consistent only with Hindu presuppositions, and not with the reality of the world as it is. To bring a Hindu believer to Christ, that had to be exposed. Simply appealing to a religious experience would not be enough for someone who had wallowed in the mystical experiences of the East.

We learnt that some people have to reach absolute rock bottom before they can be helped and that it is impossible to bring someone to God before he is ready to come. People often ask us why, with so many unsaved youngsters in America, we travelled so far from home to talk about Jesus. The simple answer is that in the jails and the slimy hotels, the dirty hospitals and the back-alley gutters, young people hit bottom with a jolt that makes them realise suddenly that they need something outside of themselves. Lying on the bottom, they look up - and see God. We wanted to be there when they needed help to get back onto their feet.

The difficult period when we were plagued by deceivers in our early days in Kabul taught us important lessons, principles that have served me all my years in ministry since then. They stopped me and others from wasting countless hours and endless effort in painful giving out to those who weren't really interested.

We discovered that we had to be more discerning - to see beyond the outward actions and words and identify what was going on under the surface. Not every person who came to us asking for help had been sent by God. Some were simply insincere, trying to take advantage of us - and get a meal, a bed, or some money. Others were actually sent by Satan himself - though they may not have been aware of it - to take up our time, our energy, and the limited physical space that we had. While we were busy with these folk, those who were more needy and potentially more open to our help were being missed.

In responding to this challenge, we realised that we could not let the pressure of people's needs determine who we ministered to. Just because someone came to us with awful, desperate needs didn't mean - hard as it may sound - that we were necessarily the people to try to meet those needs. In other words, we learnt that the need is not automatically the call. If that were the case, then *all* Christians should be in India, or Ethiopia, or wherever the latest terrible disaster area is.

We prayed about each person we met and God gave us clear supernatural guidance about which people we were to get involved with. I believe that this deep dependence on God's guidance is one of the reasons that so many people who became Christians in Afghanistan are still in some form of Christian service today.

God also showed us where to channel our energies through a practical screening process. When someone came to us they would be welcomed in by stages. First they might come for a drink of tea, then we would invite them back for a meal. After that we would ask them to spend a day with us, and only then would we consider inviting them to come and live with us.

Initially this testing of people's sincerity cut against the grain of my normally trusting personality. But we began to see how important it was to know that the people we were dealing with had been sent by God - and that making a seeker prove his sincerity didn't have to indicate to him that we didn't love him.

Some of those people we were involved with had such deep needs that they could take up the energies of four or five people, so we found that it was very important for a team to work together so that there was less likelihood of our being manipulated.

We learnt also that it was very important for us, as Christians, to keep control of the "spiritual atmosphere" in our community. Sometimes one non-Christian could ruin the whole atmosphere, and yet at other times we could have many more non-believers around but because they were open and sincere they would not tip the balance. We wanted a Christian environment of love and respect for one another.

It was difficult to gain wisdom so that we were not manipulated by people's needs, and sometimes those with the greatest needs were the most manipulative. Folk like Chris, the suicidal junkie, thrived on pity - and, like others, would threaten to kill himself if we didn't help. Desperately concerned about this issue we went to prayer. We came to the conclusion that God was telling us that in these situations we did not have ultimate responsibility for a person's life; we did not have to respond as though blackmailed. We believed God told us that the ultimate responsibility for a life lay with the person himself. He was the one who would have to give account to God.

We called this "tough love". To teach people to accept responsibility, it was sometimes necessary to say "No".

God loved them so much that He had created them with free will, and their decisions were their own.

For those who were struggling to get free from some deep emotional and spiritual bondage, it sometimes took a long time for them to reach this understanding. In the meantime, we had to go on loving them patiently, showing real concern and interest. We saw that it was through unconditional love - through committed relationships and friendships - that people became secure enough to grow and change. So many people had been hurt - by authority figures or by their parents - that they needed time to respond to love. Sometimes many months would pass before they would really open up their lives, and let us know about their hurts and fears. But time and again we saw the healing power of love which could win through and bring about miraculous changes when all else had failed. We came to appreciate that this kind of love - the love of Calvary with no barriers - was the most powerful tool that God has given us as Christians.

Another vitally important lesson was about spiritual warfare. We realised that in dealing with needy people we would come into contact with spiritual powers of evil that were trying to destroy their lives. We knew that if we didn't take seriously the nature of the conflict in which we were engaged, then we too could become targets and victims of the spiritual forces at work in the lives of those we were trying to help.

Coupled with all this was a powerful, growing awareness of the dynamism of prayer. Over and over again when we had come to the end of our abilities, ideas and strength, God encouraged and enabled us through prayer.

We didn't realise how essential these lessons would be in the even more demanding situations that God was leading us into, in a city closer to home geographically, but in its own way even further from Him.

Fifteen

Two of Every Kind

Six of us set out from Afghanistan to establish our "bridgehead" back in Europe. There were Sally and I, our fifteen month old daughter Misha, and three members of the Dilaram team - Carol Saia, and Ron and Jan McGaughy. From some of the people we met in Kabul, Ron and Jan learned about a twenty year old bus that had been converted into a home-made camper, complete with double bed, bunks, dining area and sink. It was for sale at a remarkably cheap price. Only after Ron and Jan had gone to Austria to buy it from the owners did they discover why - it broke down twenty-five times on the way back to Kabul!

Before dawn one November morning we piled all our worldly possessions on top of the old vehicle, strapped them down with a heavy-duty tarpaulin, and turned to say an emotional farewell. A seventy-strong crowd had gathered to wave us off, comprising the rest of our co-workers in Kabul who would be staying on to lead the work, members of the Kabul Christian Community Church who over the months had become our dear friends and supporters, folk from the diplomatic corps and the embassies with whom we had worked closely, and a few travellers we knew well. With a final flurry of hugs and handshakes, we piled aboard the bus, started the engine - and nothing happened! Our grand departure turned into a laughing circus as we unceremoniously struggled to push start a ten ton bus.

We left Afghanistan with mixed feelings. Although we were looking forward to our new venture in Amsterdam, we had felt very much at home in Kabul, which made it difficult to leave knowing that we might not be able to return. Sally in particular loved the bleak barren beauty of the country and when we had the chance we loved to go up to the mountains just outside the city, especially the Khyber Pass which had a majestic splendour. We knew Amsterdam would be so different.

An hour after we left Kabul, the bus broke down on the edge of town and we had to replace the generator before finally setting off again on the Trail. It only broke down once more as we snaked our way up through Iran, Turkey, Yugoslavia and across central Europe. We soon discovered that the nausea from which Sally had suffered since stepping into the shabby green bus wasn't entirely due to the bumpy ride on rough-and-ready roads, or the wafts of diesel fumes that belched in through the windows from time to time.

Our second child was on the way! With the restrictions of cramped travelling conditions, it was a miserable journey for Sally, and trying to keep Misha occupied wasn't easy either! To make matters worse, after an overnight stop at a Greek camping ground, Misha came down with a terrible fever and rash. When we called in at a German YWAM base we were warned that it could be german measles, and a potential threat to our unborn baby. Reluctantly, we left Misha with Ron and Jan - who were staying on at the base to try to unblock the bus's frozen piping - and flew the final stage of our trek to Amsterdam.

Six weeks after we boarded the ex-hippy bus back in Afghanistan, we jumped out of another battered old van that had collected us at Holland's Schipol Airport and dropped us right on the quay by the houseboats, about which we had prayed so long and hard, and for which we had so many hopes and dreams.

I was excited as I sensed the new work God was leading us into, but I could tell the slump of emotions in Sally as we looked at the two boats, chained together in the murky water.

The name - "The Ark" - seemed appropriate because it had been home at some time or other for at least two of every kind! But right then it looked as though Noah and his party had just left. A small team had remained on board after the summer work was finished, but they had understandably not done anything in launching a permanent ministry because they weren't sure what it was going to be used for. I had hoped that we might live in a nice home once back in the West so my heart sank as low as Sally's when they showed us our living area on the boat - one small room, admittedly in relatively good condition, right next to the main kitchen and dining area. It was going to be a squeeze for Sally, Misha and me - and what about the addition to our family? I recognised that The Ark would remain a permanent pain in the neck for me in at least one sense - houseboats were not designed with tall basketball players in mind!

There was worse to follow below decks. Formerly used as a boarding school for seamen's children, the boats had seen far better days and were in a generally poor state of repair. One of them was simply an enormous dormitory which had served as the sleeping quarters for about one hundred children. Down the centre of the lower deck ran a long row of stone hand-basins, with a bewildering network of pipes and ducting so that it looked like a giant piece of modern art, or a huge cattle trough. The boys' and girls' sections were separated by no more than a thin partition across the centre and to make it worse the beds were all child-sized and totally unsuitable for adults.

Suddenly the Olfat seemed more like a four-star hotel than I had ever thought possible, and I wondered how as a growing family we were going to cope with living in such miserable conditions. There might not be the primitiveness of life in the East to contend with, I thought, but there were the headaches of substandard Western civilisation. After just a few minutes below deck, we were aware of the dramatic changes in climate we would have to get used to, switching from the heat of Afghanistan to a European winter. Sitting below the water line, the interior of the boat was cold and damp, and even non-stop heating failed to take the edge off the chill.

Sally had been so thankful when we finally arrived in Amsterdam, but as soon as she stepped off the quay onto the nearest boat, she realised that her thankfulness had been premature. She had simply traded the bouncing of the old bus for the gentler rocking of the boat, neither of which were conducive to a pleasant pregnancy! A few nights later, she quietly asked God to show her His favour by taking away the awful sickness. She would go anywhere, do anything, endure any situation, she told Him, but she did need to be healthy if she was going to cope.

Within twenty-four hours, the dreadful nausea passed.

Ron and Jan McGaughy joined us with Misha a week after our arrival and of course we could hardly wait to be re-united with our daughter. Doctors had confirmed that she didn't have german measles, thankfully, but the wrong initial diagnosis meant that the scarlet fever from which she was suffering hadn't been diagnosed as soon as it might have been. As a result, she suffered its effects for three long months. The demands of a normally lively, now invalided, toddler were just more pressures on Sally as she tried to establish a new home for us.

Some of the folk who had stayed on board until our arrival had different ideas about the boats' future from ours. There were suggestions that they should be used as a centre for smuggling Bibles into Eastern Europe, a hospitality centre for sailors, or a Christian youth hostel. They were unaware of the work we had been doing in Kabul, and that we had come to Amsterdam to extend what had been started there.

After two exasperating months of caution and getting used to our new environment, I took the bull by the horns. I called a meeting and announced firmly: "We are going to use the boats as a halfway house for people in trouble here in Amsterdam." It broke the impasse, and The Ark became the focus for all sorts of wonderful outreach to the drop-outs who drifted into the city from all over Europe.

A tremendous amount of work went into not only making the boats ship-shape, but also creating a warm, easy-going atmosphere where people could feel welcome and comfortable. It took a determined team of hefty volunteers several days to dismantle the monstrous washstands in the dormitory and once they had been hacked away, we divided the huge floorspace into smaller rooms for between four and six people to share.

Soon after our arrival in Amsterdam, we discovered that it was normal for people living in the city to dump furniture and fittings which they no longer required at the side of the road for the refuse men. There were some rich pickings, including quality cast-offs. A few early-morning runs along the route the refuse collectors would soon be following provided all the chairs, tables, settees, carpeting and lights we needed to equip The Ark as a new home for people who needed help.

Soon there was a regular stream of visitors, many of them needing special help, and we were as busy as we had been in Kabul. But despite the encouraging signs, and the swiftness with which we seemed to be established, spiritually those early days in Amsterdam were difficult ones, particularly for us as a family unit.

We knew God had called us to The Ark, and looking back on the chain of events which had led us there confirmed it. Although I found it a difficult time, I didn't fully appreciate how Sally was feeling. After a few months of intense work and activity, I was pulled up sharp when I realised that in my determination to see The Ark established in its new work, I had actually forgotten many of the principles about commitment to God, family and ministry that I had learnt during our winter separation in Afghanistan. Sally was going through a period of depression: I had not been sensitive enough to her needs and she had not felt able to share her thoughts with me.

I then made a point of easing up on my involvement in the daily running of The Ark. While the rest of the community met for breakfast, had personal quiet times and then did the chores - maintenance, laundry, cooking, cleaning - around the boats, Sally, Misha and I had time together. This became a routine which greatly helped our family over the years. Mid-morning we joined the others for our "Ark family" time of praise, worship and Bible study. After lunch there were groups going out into the city to make further contacts with needy young people, some of whom were invited back for the evening meal.

That meant that the tiny dining room was always packed tight to over-flowing with between forty and fifty people. At other times we counselled people more personally. On the boat alongside when the open coffee bar was in full swing, upwards of one hundred people would squeeze inside regularly to meet friends, talk, listen to music and relax with tea or coffee.

Misha, who had been independent from birth and enjoyed exploring and dashing around, was anxious to know everything that was going on. Sally was constantly fearful that she might topple overboard. Misha needed continual "policing" by Sally or one of the team, and as Sally grew larger, her agility in getting around the cramped decks and walkways diminished. To make matters worse Sally had more responsibilities when we bought a little black mongrel dog. We had always loved animals and missed Smack, our boxer, who we had left behind in Kabul with the team in Dilaram House as he was very settled there. The idea was that our new pet, Frodo, would be a friend and guard-dog, and also be a way of introducing Misha to the competition for people's affection, as a baby brother or sister would soon be arriving on the scene. Frodo was a bit wild and fell overboard several times in the beginning. He didn't come to any harm but had to be bathed, as the canal water stank!

Once the general accommodation was sorted out, we arranged for two small apartments to be erected on the top floor of the boat nearest to the pier. We had the larger one, and while it was cramped in the extreme - the three small rooms probably covered less floorspace than the average lounge - it did give us some "family space" away from the pressure cooker atmosphere of the small dorms and rooms on the other boat. There was only one spiral staircase leading down to the decks, though, at the far end from our rooms. So whenever we needed to go to the bathroom, we had to negotiate something of an obstacle course.

While Sally was struggling to deal with all the changes in our circumstances, I was close to being overwhelmed myself by the new work and all its extra responsibilities. From heading up a small, fairly tight-knit work in Kabul with a total of around thirty, I was now trying to establish a work with a live-in capacity of almost sixty. A coffee bar was running every night in the boat beneath our living quarters, and outreach teams worked every afternoon in the parks, streets and hotels around the city. Some would bring their day's contacts to the Sunday night teaching and praise meetings.

We were not only ministering to those who came to The Ark for help, but also discipling and encouraging members of the team. Many of them were young Christians - some no more than six or nine months old in their faith. Looking back, it seems almost foolhardy to have placed such inexperienced people in such responsible roles, but at the time there was no alternative, and all those of us who were involved recognised God's special grace in protecting and guiding us.

Our location might have changed, but our philosophy was just the same. In many ways we made The Ark a "floating Dilaram". We went out into the city in pairs, striking up conversations with young people in the youth hostels and hotels, or at the popular rallying points for hippies, drop-outs and junkies - the centrally-located Dam Square, or the spacious Vondel Park. If they were interested, we invited them back for coffee, and from there continued to try to build relationships, seeking to share the gospel naturally through the friendships we were making. We invited them back for longer periods before finally asking them to come and live as part of the community, if they showed a real desire to discover more about Christ.

We felt that wherever a person stood spiritually - be it atheist, agnostic, backslider, or "nominal" Christian - our goal was simply to help them move nearer to Jesus. Not necessarily all the way, in one sudden jump, but closer than they were.

If a person's understanding of the truth of the Gospel could be expressed on a scale somewhere between zero and one hundred, with the latter representing salvation, then they could be anywhere along that register. The goal of evangelism should be to discover where people are - say, at forty-five - and then help them move closer to conversion. But that doesn't always happen at one time. Trying to force people to believe or listen to something they do not want to receive can do more harm than good.

We believed that people needed to be drawn to Jesus through our sharing the truth in love and friendship - in the way He did when on earth. So it was that The Ark was regularly visited by drop-outs, runaways and other alienated young people, sitting round sipping tea and coffee and drinking in the atmosphere of love and friendship - both of which were hard to find on the harsh streets outside.

It was this gentle witness that made The Ark such an appropriate name for a place where people could find some shelter from the storms that were battering them. Over the years, countless people have come to faith in Christ through the patient, persistent love of The Ark community.

When Sally was eight months pregnant, we felt the Lord again confirming that we were in the place He wanted, even though living conditions were difficult. During the night, Sally fell down the iron steps in the darkness on the way to the bathroom. She was shaken, as we all were, but amazingly she soon recovered. We felt her safety was an indication from God that He wanted us there and would take care of us despite the problems, if only we trusted Him.

Although Sally's physical health was good, psychologically she was feeling low, and functioning as if under a cloud. The adjustment to settling down in a new place, having a lively toddler to care for and being pregnant, all at the same time, was a lot to cope with. Despite this, she managed to create a warm atmosphere on the boats.

During that period Sally had to cope with new feelings of insecurity. It was a traumatic time for her but she said afterwards that she had learnt so much both about herself and about the Lord that she was grateful to Him for putting her in this situation. When she was working her way through it though, she was emotionally drained and we wondered if this style of communal living really was right for us. I knew I had to make my own family a priority and give more time to them. Sally and Misha needed it. Not long after our arrival in Amsterdam, it came home to Sally and me how unusual our family life in Kabul had been when we visited a park on the outskirts of the city.

Misha exclaimed, "Mommy, Daddy, what's that?"

We looked and couldn't see anything. "What do you mean, Misha?"

"That over there," she said, pointing to the ground. Sally and I realised Misha was pointing at the grass. She didn't know what grass was! Was it wrong for us as a family to live in such extreme circumstances? Though we often asked ourselves that question, and in spite of the difficulties we had faced, we had a growing awareness of the rich lessons we were learning together. We saw, with increasing concern, the superficiality of others around us and we came to appreciate the depth God was bringing to our lives.

We also began to realise that there was a desperate need for many more families to do what we were doing. We did not begrudge the sacrifices we had made. In fact, we rejoiced because of all that we had learnt and experienced. We only wished many more families would do the same.

We believed that it was fundamentally important to have a fairly strict schedule, because having older Christians, those who were new in their faith, and non-believers with serious needs all living together was not easy. Discipling became a natural way of life, rather then just a formula. We learnt and grew together as a Christian community, as we shared closely in each other's lives and needs.

This sense of family was especially evident the night

that Matthew was born. We had planned for a home delivery in the same way that Misha had arrived out in Kabul, but we had to change these plans at the last minute when the midwife unexpectedly went on vacation. So Sally went into hospital to give birth, but she was determined to be home as soon as possible with our new baby. There were no complications, so the doctors allowed her and Matthew home within just a couple of hours - on the condition that she had to be brought home in an ambulance. We happily agreed - but there were some heart-stopping moments on the way.

The ambulancemen had to carry her on board The Ark on a stretcher! At one stage, as they hauled her up and round the spiral staircase to our flat, Sally was hanging vertically in the stretcher. I was thankful that she was well strapped in - and greatly relieved that they soon had her eased round the staircase and tucked up in our bedroom without my visions of her being dropped overboard having become a reality.

Within moments of my tucking the two of them up in bed together, there was a gentle tap on the door. I opened it, and the first of a procession of young people made their way into the tiny room to say hello to their adoptive baby brother. We thought back to the night Misha was born and were thrilled to share these special moments with them. It was a reminder that we had been called as a family to this work - that we all had to sacrifice our privacy, and some of our time together, to be available to those we had come to help. We couldn't just shut the door behind us at five o'clock and say: "See you tomorrow." We were living "over the shop", which often meant being available twenty-four hours a day and seven days a week.

There were setbacks and failures in our work on The Ark and sometimes we struggled with people for weeks only to see them slip back into their old ways, returning to their addictions and the probability of bleak futures. At these times, despite our despair and frustration at such unresponsiveness, we had to trust God for their lives. We were painfully reminded time and again that although God's loving arms will reach out to gather in anyone who wants to run to them, those same people can deliberately choose to step beyond His grasp.

Work on The Ark brought us into direct conflict with the forces of evil, as we had experienced in Afghanistan. Sometimes the spiritual struggle in which we were involved manifested itself in open aggression and attacks against us. During the years the boats were home to our community, there were numerous threats of violence to workers and damage to property. Fights would break out occasionally among those visiting the coffee bar - some of whom could be strung out on drugs and drink - requiring courageous and firm handling by the men on the team.

On one occasion I confronted a Dutch youth who had been on board as part of our community for only a few days. It had soon become clear that he wasn't seriously interested in finding out more about Christianity; in fact he was using the boats as a drug-dealing base. I challenged him bluntly, and reminded him of our house rules. He was incensed at my accusations, and started to shout and swear loudly at me, threatening all manner of dire consequences if we insisted he leave. Finally I calmly told one of the other team members, "We've tried to explain things reasonably to him. Go and telephone the police."

The young man I'd spoken to turned to go to the 'phone, at which point the addict leapt onto his back and started to attack him. It wasn't a time for easy words. I grabbed him by the shoulders, dragged him off, threw him onto the floor and dropped my knee into the small of his back. After a few minutes' snarling, his breathing returned to normal, and he agreed to leave quietly. As he went he warned over his shoulder that he would be back for revenge.

It was more an act of bravado than a threat we took seriously - unlike a similar situation that was to arise not much later.

Two guys arrived at the coffee bar one night and soon expressed an interest in moving into the community. Virtually within hours we had discerned their reasons - they were big-time drug pushers and distributors, and thought that the loving, caring, peacemaking environment of The Ark would make a perfect cover for their operations. I had to ask them to leave, firmly but politely. This time, though, I took the precaution of ensuring that half a dozen of the male workers were around as our interview took place. It was just as well.

They pulled a wicked-looking knife and jabbed it at me menacingly as one of them warned angrily: "Your kids won't be able to walk the streets safely from now on. You won't be able to stop looking back over your shoulder for a minute, because you won't know when we are coming to get you!"

This was a serious threat, we felt, and "guard duties" were assigned for several nights after their departure before we felt we were safe because their anger had subsided and they had moved on to new pastures.

These times were frightening, and they demanded responsible handling: after all, we had women and children on board. Even so, these threats didn't make us want to shy away from our uncompromising stand. We believed that it was fundamentally important to have few rules governing our lifestyle at The Ark - but that those we did make should be kept. We had to exercise the "tough love" we had learnt to develop in Afghanistan - at times calling people's bluff, even demanding that some leave.

Nor did we feel that we could shy away from situations that might bring us into possible conflict. One such occasion developed when some of The Ark workers got involved with the wife of the leader of the Hare Krishna temple in the city. She had turned to our people for help, and through their love and concern had renounced her eastern faith and become a Christian. It was an understandably explosive decision.

When he learnt about what had happened, the woman's husband thundered down to the harbour and screamed at Peter Fitzgerald, who was then leading The Ark work: "If you every try to help my wife again, I will splatter the blood of you and your children all over the sides of this boat!"

We were aware that the boats were at the centre of fierce spiritual warfare and all of us, young and old alike, were in the front line.

Such confrontations are not unlike those described in the Bible in the lives of David, Joseph, Abraham, Paul, Peter and many others. I had often prayed that I would learn to be a man of God - to fear Him and not fear man - so could I complain when God took me up on my prayer?

Sally and I believed that God wanted to use our family to touch the lives of many people for Him. We knew we could do nothing less than give Him our all, even if it meant sacrifice. Thought it was sometimes difficult, we had many rewards and we often felt sorry for those who had to live a "normal life"!

Sixteen

Changed by Chance?

What the world sees as coincidences I believe are divine appointments. Ostensibly casual encounters with non-Christians can be used by God to expose them for the first time to His truth and perhaps stimulate them to further thought about spiritual issues, or maybe seal their salvation with the convicting and healing work of His Spirit.

None of the YWAM leaders in Amsterdam hold this certainty more strongly than John Goodfellow - and with good reason.

He was an alcoholic drug addict with a ready recourse to violence and a confused spiritual hunger that was driving him on a strange mystical quest to the East - if the law didn't catch up with him - when a seemingly chance meeting led him to The Ark, to God, and to an unexpected new life and purpose.

To this day he grins, shakes his head with near-disbelief at the way it all happened, and tells delightedly of the dramatic intervention.

By the time he arrived in Amsterdam, he had slipped a long way from the outwardly respectable lifestyle in which he had been raised in Nottingham, one of England's many light-industrial towns. Church attendance every Sunday was a family custom, but for John his faith had nothing to do with life during the rest of the week. He even served as an altar boy for several years, ritually donning his robes, but with no understanding beyond a youthful acceptance that this was a tedious but harmless custom that kept family and friends in the community happy. By his late teens even that motivation wasn't enough, and when he left school to begin work as an apprentice brick-layer he took his move to "adulthood" as a time to demonstrate his independence by refusing to attend church any more.

The dropping of this lip service to convention seemed to open a previously closed side of his personality, and John began to live completely for himself. By Monday morning, Friday's wage packet was spent on socialising in pubs and clubs. The thirst for drink and the lavish high-life soon demanded more cash than he had so John turned unquestioningly to crime.

Radios, cameras, coats, handbags and other saleable items were snatched from cars and sold cheaply for ready money. The pickings were not rich enough for long though, and in the early hours one morning John graduated to harder crime when he rammed an iron bar through a jeweller's shop window and sprinted off down the street with his pockets bulging with watches, rings, lockets and precious stones.

His bravado outstripped his planning and within fifteen minutes he had been overtaken by police with tracker dogs. He ended up in court with a two-year probation order, but this setback wasn't enough to make John reconsider his ways. He continued with petty theft and even the occasional mugging to finance his nights out. At twenty, John travelled to Europe as a newly-qualified master bricklayer where his skills were in high demand.

In Spain he met up with a group of friends who were working in a large discotheque at one of the popular coastal resorts. He was taken on the staff, and drifted between duties as a waiter, doorman and disc jockey. The excitement of the nightlife and the opportunities for no-strings-attached relationships with girls away for a fortnight's sunshine and holiday romance soon led him into taking drugs for the first time, in addition to his continual heavy drinking.

"It wasn't unusual for me to be so 'wired' that I'd be wide awake, energetic and lively, for two to three days at a stretch," he remembers. "Then I'd collapse into a dead sleep for twenty-four hours; then start all over again."

Soon he was experimenting with LSD, and to finance his own habit he turned to crime - this time dealing in pills and marijuana with many of the club guests.

Violence was an accepted part of the scene, and if there weren't brawls and fights erupting spontaneously within the large crowd of "good time" holidaymakers which required sorting out by John and his friends, then in their crazier moments it wasn't unknown for them to provoke some action themselves! Bottles, stones and knives would fly as the fighting spilled out onto the streets. He thrived on aggression and pain.

John spent his summers in this mindless haze, and returned home for the winter months, bricklaying where necessary, or doing other jobs like being a waiter at a stylish Swiss hotel, where he stayed long enough to discover that he didn't have the personality suited for such a humble role, so he stole several hundred pounds' worth of wine and other hotel property before leaving.

On one of his autumn trips to England, John came through Amsterdam to investigate the hippy capital of Europe, about which he had heard so much. Travelling without his usual supply of speed, for fear of being detained at the border, and soon suffering without his daily intake, John's impressions of the city were clouded by a paralysing attack of paranoia. Even though his pockets were bulging with ready cash, he didn't dare walk into a hotel and ask for a room. Instead, unwashed and wild-eyed, he spent the night out in the open, by the river near the centre of the city. He left Amsterdam hurriedly the next day, determined never to return to the place where he had felt so uncomfortable and ill at ease.

Back in England, John developed a successful insurance fraud involving false claims for baggage supposedly lost while travelling. It was simple, and he easily netted sums of three hundred and four hundred pounds each time. A small enough amount to escape suspicion, but enough to provide plenty of drugs and drink, which by this time were really taking their toll. Heavy use of speed left him forgetful and uncommunicative - and unreliable for regular work. He was forced more and more into crime to make money.

In a rare moment of rationality, John took stock of his life. He was twenty-five, strung out on drugs and alcohol, increasingly caught in a web of violence, crime and meaningless encounters with a succession of women. Somehow it didn't have the glamour of his earlier years.

One day he saw an advertisement in the newspapers for bricklayers needed in Canada. With unexpected resolve he applied for and got one of the jobs, determined that this overseas trip would be the chance to put the past well behind him and settle down to earning an honest day's pay. The money was certainly good, and life in Canada seemed to offer enough for a young man to manage without the crutches of speed and booze.

But it wasn't to be. Within three weeks, John was dealing in dope, using speed heavily once more, and downing almost a bottle of brandy a day. His physical condition was so poor that he was only capable of working a couple of days each week - just about enough to pay for his rent and food. The dream of a new start had ended, followed by a nightmare about the reality of his situation.

"I woke up in a cold sweat one morning and sat bolt

upright. It just sank home that I was lost - a shell of a man with no meaning to his life, heading nowhere. It was a frightening thought. All that I'd thought would give a meaning to life - fast cars, hard drinking, free sex - was empty and worthless."

The terrifying awareness of his inner emptiness propelled John into a desperate search for reality. On his return to England he linked up with a former junkie friend who was now heavily immersed in the occult.

Here perhaps was meaning, John thought, so he began to explore for himself. He read extensively, investigated astrology and tarot, and many other forms of the Black Arts. Finally he decided that, yes, there was a God: and that the secret of communion with Him lay in the mountain ranges of the Middle East.

John believed that his now all-consuming search for "truth" would be over once he found his way out to the Dervishes, a mystical cult of tribesmen who roamed the remote highlands of the ancient land of Persia, now Iran. There he would spend the rest of his life riding with the men whom he believed held the secret of the universe, and who through secret rituals could get him in touch with the life force he was seeking.

His intensity won over three friends who were also looking for a deeper meaning to life, and the four intended to buy an old touring van and travel overland to Iran from Europe. But the venture required money they didn't have, so a planned series of further frauds brought John and his new partners in crime back to Amsterdam. Things did not go as he planned!

John's first fraud worked sweetly, as it always had done, but there was a delay in setting up the further ones needed to finance the trip. The gang booked in at a Christian youth hostel in the Red Light District, where there was cheap accommodation and good food. The four men stayed there for a few days, supplementing their income with some further petty crimes, while they finalised their plans.

One evening they were attracted by a poster on the wall of the hostel to hear a live band playing at a club called The Ark, which they had not heard of before. When they arrived they were sorely disappointed to discover that neither the drugs nor the alcohol with which they had hoped to pass the next few hours were available. They were impressed enough by the music to stay around though, and make do with the freely-available soft drinks.

John's interest perked up when an attractive young girl came over to talk to him. But his expectations were shattered when she began in a friendly and unaffected way to talk to him about Jesus Christ, the Son of God, through whom people could come into a relationship with the creator of the whole universe! Embarrassed, surprised and confused, John quickly made his excuses and left. He found his way to one of the nightclubs he had previously learnt supplied Amsterdam's youth culture, and tried to put the unsettling conversation on The Ark out of his mind with an excess of drink and drugs.

That brief exchange of words shook him more than he realised so the next morning the gang decided to wait no longer, but move on from Amsterdam to complete their frauds elsewhere.

They were just tidying up their arrangements at a public pay 'phone at the Central Station, when who should walk right past them but Sherry, the girl with whom they had spoken the night before. Arriving at The Ark, just a few hundred yards away, she had realised that she had left her purse behind at her lodgings, and was on her way back to retrieve it when she bumped into John and his accomplices.

Seemingly unaware of, or certainly unruffled by, their awkwardness, she invited them to join her for something to eat at a nearby cafe. Their hunger, through dwindling funds, overcame their suspicions. During their lunch together, Sherry once more began to talk openly and unassumingly about the man-God she said had risen from death to bring freedom and forgiveness into the world. This time the four men were won over by her warmth and genuineness, and were curious to know more so, when she invited them onto The Ark that evening for a meal, they eagerly accepted.

Over that meal, John was moved by the sensitivity and concern of the people in the community, and the faith they expressed so surely. He and his friends later agreed that these people "had something" - and that they would stay around, after all, until they found out what it was! For the next few days they returned regularly for food and company. "I kept a really close eye on all the people who worked at The Ark. I was convinced that they had to be on something to be so loving, peaceful and calm - especially in view of some of the agitated people they had to deal with! I was determined to spot the bottle of pills they were passing round and find out what they were; they had to be good!" John confessed later.

Finally the four men moved onto The Ark, and one day soon afterwards John admitted that he had become convinced of the reality of the God about whom we spoke - he had seen His existence in our lives. But it was to be another fortnight of patient and gentle witnessing before he could accept that this same God had sent His only Son into the world to ransom John Goodfellow from all his wickedness, through His death on the cross.

The breakthrough came quietly and simply during one of our community times of praise and worship. John broke down and began to weep as God's Spirit revealed the depths of his sinfulness, and the endless reach of His own redeeming love. The mixed-up addict, who had always been able to justify even his most vicious and selfish behaviour, recognised that the time for excuses was over.

Later than night, by his bed in one of the small rooms below the waterline, he knelt down beside his mattress. In the quietness, as the water lapped against the hull, he whispered: "Oh, God, for the first time in my life I see what a wicked person I am. Please come into my life, Jesus, and help me, forgive me God." During the next few weeks, John explained that he had repeated that simple request three or four times each night, "just to make sure".

If ever there was any doubt that his prayer had been answered, John experienced a profound infilling of the Spirit, sweeping away instantly his craving for alcohol, drugs and tobacco. In its place was released another passionate thirst - to know more of, and about, God. John began to devour his Bible.

In the days that followed John poured out the sorrowful story of his past to me. Although our discipling included teaching about the need for restitution - putting right the past so that God can lead powerfully into the future - I didn't push him on this point right away. I wanted to wait, for I sensed that God would bring John to this realisation soon Himself. I wasn't wrong.

One day John came to me with a letter he had received from a friend back home in Nottingham. The police were looking for him in connection with an insurance fraud.

"I've got to go back and face up to it," he told me with a certainty in his voice.

"I know," I answered simply and thankfully.

There followed one of the strangest Continental telephone conversations the Nottingham constabulary have probably ever received - a young man ringing from a boat in Amsterdam harbour telling them that he had become a Christian, and was coming back to admit to a crime he had so far got away with.

As he prepared to return home, I commended John for his decision, and assured him that there were people in the area we knew with whom we could put him in touch.

Good, solid Christians, who would help him nourish the strong roots he was putting down into God. They would love him and support has as we would if we could be there.

John was astonished. "You mean - there are more people like you?" he asked in genuine amazement.

"Why, yes. What do you mean, John?"

"Well, you know, real Christians. People who know God personally in the way you do here on The Ark. I've been around the world a bit, and I've never come across anyone who really knows Jesus like you before. I thought that you must be the only real Christians there were..."

I didn't know whether to smile at John's innocence, or weep at the sad truth revealed by his ignorance. How had he seen so much and been so far without ever having been spoken to by a Christian before?

If it hadn't been for Sherry's mislaid purse, John might never have heard about Jesus. He could have been chasing a wild dream in the Iranian mountains. Instead he was doing something that observers might have thought equally strange - freely returning to face an almost certain prison sentence.

John and his four friends, who had also become Christians, packed their bags and got ready to catch the ferry knowing that the police were waiting to take them into custody on the British side. I was completely unaware at that time that John Goodfellow would be a key figure in all that was to happen later in our ministry in Amsterdam.

Seventeen

Who Can You Trust?

We had only been on The Ark for a few months when I was reminded of something that had struck me years previously; the need for a proper training centre where people could be prepared effectively for service. After all, I figured, if the United States spent so much money in training its soldiers, shouldn't God's army consider such an investment of time and expertise important, too?

But the rather cramped and often crisis-ridden conditions on The Ark did not lend themselves to its use as a training base. We needed somewhere away from the direct heat of the battle where our "troops" could be properly "drilled", "equipped" and receive their individual orders.

Romkje de Graaf, who for several years had acted as travelling companion and aide to Corrie Ten Boom, had been involved with the work of YWAM since its earliest days in the Netherlands. Now I asked her to comb all the property columns of the newspapers for a suitable property that could house one hundred people or so.

It was a long time before she found anything, but then, one day, she came across an advertisement for a small estate standing in two hectares of land practically adjacent to the German border. The day we were due to visit it, Romkje suddenly remembered another place, about an hour-and-a-half's drive north of Amsterdam, which seemed suitable. It was a former leprosy hospital, with a number of outbuildings, but she had not thought of mentioning it before because a businessman friend was in the process of buying it to turn it into a Christian conference centre.

Still, we decided to check it over. Set in beautiful pasturelands and forests right on the edge of the national park, Heidebeek was ideal. In addition to offices and lecture rooms, there was accommodation for one hundred and twenty-five people. After hearing from Romkje's acquaintance that he was unable to pursue his plans because of a lack of finance, and visiting the other property, which turned out to fall far short of our expectations, we prayed and fasted over Heidebeek for a week after reporting back to The Ark community.

At the end of that time we felt that God wanted us to buy Heidebeek. The only drawback was that it was on the market for 475,000 guilders. And we didn't have any money whatsoever. Indeed we didn't even have enough to keep the Ark going on a day-to-day basis. Often we would be out of food, as in Afghanistan, only to find supplies of meat and vegetables left on the quayside by well-wishers and supporters.

Undaunted, we contacted the owners and declared our interest in purchasing the estate. Then we prayed about it again, and sat back confidently waiting for the guilders to drop from heaven. They didn't come! Finally we decided to approach a bank for help. We caused considerable amusement as we turned up in our customary fashions - long hair and hippy garb - to ask for such a large loan.

In our increasingly anxious search for the money we needed, I didn't have the time to reflect on the changes that had taken place over the years. Here was the guy who was once too "straight" to be accepted by the hippies he wanted to work with, who was now too "way out" for the conservative business folk with whom he really had more in common! I'm sure that God found time to smile over it though.

Perhaps not surprisingly, we didn't find our bank loan. But meanwhile the owners of the property were in regular contact, asking for a meeting to discuss the contract.

"Could you bear with us just a little while?" I stalled. "We'd like to talk this through thoroughly with our financial advisors."

They seemed happy enough with this - little realising I had in mind Father, Son and Holy Spirit! A couple of weeks later they telephoned again, and once more I begged extra time to talk with our "advisors". I felt that I couldn't tell them straight out that we didn't have a penny, so we prayed that the money would somehow be given to us.

A little while later, with still no progress in raising the necessary funds, I read in one of the newspapers that Heidebeek had been sold! We were badly disappointed, but accepted that the owners had not wanted to be kept hanging around any longer. Yet we had been so sure that this had been the place that God intended for us, and now it had gone. What had we done wrong? Where had we failed Him?

A few weeks later while I was over in the States, I met up with Joy Dawson, a close friend who had supported and encouraged us in our work since our earliest days in Afghanistan. She prayed with us about Heidebeek when we first considered taking it on, and I told her that it had gone to someone else.

"Well, has the Lord told you that you are not to have it?" she asked straightforwardly.

"Er, no," I explained, a little taken aback. "We just read about it in the newspaper..."

"So who do you trust," she challenged me bluntly, "the Lord, or the newspapers?"

"But suppose somebody really has bought it?" I

protested. "What do we do then?"

"Well, then you can buy it from the new owners," she replied. "Really! Did God speak to you about the place, or didn't He?"

Duly pulled up sharp, on my return to Amsterdam I met with the team and we prayed once more about Heidebeek. Then we contacted the owners again - and discovered that Heidebeek hadn't actually been sold at all - the newspaper report had got it wrong! Joy Dawson had been right after all. There were other people interested in the property, but there was no final offer as yet, and we were still free to pursue it if we could find the money.

After much prayer, I went to a well-known Christian businessman in Amsterdam who had often made charitable loans to various Christian groups in the past.

Within minutes of being ushered into his executive, panelled office I was disappointed. He told me that one of his last loans had been to members of the Children of God. He hadn't known at the time that they were a cult, and had been devastated to learn that they were involved in drugs, sex and the occult. As a result he had stopped lending money to Christian organisations altogether.

Although I was crushed inside, we talked for another thirty minutes or so about our work on The Ark, about all that God was doing, and our plans for the future. Then, just as I was preparing to leave, he leaned over his desk.

"I will help you after all," he said reflectively. "If I got you a loan of, say, 400,000 guilders, would that help?"

"Sure," I replied, as casually as I could under the circumstances. I'd come here to ask for a loan of 75,000 guilders, been turned down flat, and now I was walking out with the promise of more than five times that!

The following day he dropped by The Ark, handed a business card to me and said: "Call this man. It's been arranged." I was impressed at the speed with which he had worked for us, and when I spoke to the bankers with whom we had been put in touch I expressed my surprise that it had been possible to make such arrangements so quickly.

"Yes, the loan's all arranged. Just come over and we'll sort out all the paperwork for you. Didn't you know that the gentleman you have been dealing with owns the bank?"

With the promise of this money, we were able to sign the contracts, and agreed to move into Heidebeek in March 1975.

Just three weeks before half of us from The Ark were due to move ashore to open up the new training centre, we added up all the bills for the houseboat operation, and were horrified to discover that they totalled 10,000 guilders. There was no way we could possibly meet them. Here we were, planning to start up a major new ministry, and we couldn't even pay the bills for the running expenses of the existing one.

After prayer, we felt that God was asking us to take an offering from among our staff on the Ark. Our philosophy was pretty straightforward - we would do the possible, and then look to God for the impossible. So eighteen out of the forty people with us at the time sold everything they had and we collected just 4,000 guilders. With only two days to go before we were due to leave, we still hadn't covered the bills.

Then, on the Friday night, at our final meeting together, one of the girls on the team said that she felt God wanted us to take another offering. "Some of us are holding out," she announced softly. It was difficult for me to call for another offering, but I sensed this was God's leading. Though many had given sacrificially, we urged those who were "holding out" to give. I was sure that if we obeyed God, He would see our faith in Him and more than meet our needs.

The next day people brought their gifts - totalling just

over 6,000 guilders. People later admitted, "We were so afraid to give the first time, because we didn't trust God. It was hard to believe that this whole thing was going to work, so we held back. We didn't think it was right to take this other place on, and we're sorry."

Through God's loving firmness we now had the money we needed to meet the bills for The Ark. But those who were moving out to Heidebeek were still planning to leave on the Monday morning with no money. Then there occurred one of those amazing answers to prayer that has become a major building stone for absolute faith in God in my life.

A visitor to our Sunday evening meeting came up to me and told me: "Yesterday afternoon, the Lord spoke to me and told me to give you some money to help you with your work...."

He handed over a cheque for 10,000 guilders!

We were staggered. Not only had God called us to selfless obedience in handing over all that we had, but He had then honoured that commitment, matching our giving to the very penny!

It was a joyful party that set out the following morning for Heidebeek. After living for eighteen months on the Ark, our move was a wonderful change for Sally. No longer did she have to be constantly on the lookout for our two inquisitive children, anxious for their safety. Even though we had managed to put a fence around the end of one of the houseboats next to our rooms so that the children could play in the fresh air, an adult always had to be in attendance as Misha was likely to climb over and fall into the foul water of the canal. Fortunately Matthew wasn't so active and adventurous. Living in a community was an advantage as often one of the young people would help Sally out if she was trying to prepare a meal or desperately needed a little time to herself. When the children needed more space to play, we took them onto

the pier, but again there was always the danger that they
would fall into the canal.

Now the children would have acres of beautiful land to
roam, fields to explore and animals to play with. The
idyllic sort of environment for children to grow up in,
away from the dangers and pressures of the city!

Although our living quarters at Heidebeek were a little
makeshift to start with, there was more space than in the
cubbyholes we had called home on The Ark. For the first
time in eight years of marriage, we had a bathroom and
kitchenette to ourselves! They were nothing fancy, but to
Sally they could have had gold-plated taps. She was
simply delighted at the space in which she could create a
more separate home for us, and the release from the
constant tensions and pressures of raising children on two
boats was wonderful.

We wanted to see Heidebeek in use as soon as possible,
so in the summer we pitched a large tent in the grounds to
stage what we called a "Kick-Off Crusade", aimed at
training four hundred young people participating in a
major YWAM campaign that would be taking place
throughout Europe. We were given permission by a
neighbouring farmer for them to camp on his land.

Not everyone was happy about our arrival in the lovely
countryside. The title of the event gave rise to suspicions
in the minds of many of the local farm folk. They were
concerned and alarmed. Wasn't "kick-off" something to
do with drugs? Was their quiet rural home about to be
invaded by an army of wild, rebellious drug addicts? Was
Heidebeek going to be turned into a centre where drug
addicts could try to come clean? We received a barrage of
anxious letters and 'phone calls.

When we realised that the residents were truly
alarmed, we visited them to explain what we were
planning, and attempted to allay their fears. They

remained sceptical, and kept a watchful eye on the comings and goings of the scores of young people who arrived for the event. The initial misunderstanding about the name turned out to be a very positive witness though, for the gathering took place peacefully. There was no rowdiness, and no litter left behind either. It made a deep impression on our quiet, conservative farming neighbours, who had been bracing themselves for the worst - an invasion of undesirable drop-outs.

Those contacts went on to pave the way for further links. We started a project to help the local farmers whenever there was an opportunity. They often welcomed a few extra pairs of hands and in one case we helped someone to re-roof his barn after the roof was torn off in a gale. Another time we were able to offer lodgings to a family when their home burned down.

Through all this development and expansion, God continued to teach us how much we needed to rely on Him totally in our work and service. If there was ever any possibility that we might forget this as, in worldly terms, our projects continued to grow successfully, He reminded us of His sovereignty and our dependence on Him.

When we took over Heidebeek, we still had to find the outstanding 75,000 guilders - which we had to pay the owners or forfeit our downpayment and lose the property. As the deadline for final payment drew nearer, the supply of money seemed to dry up. Only 15,000 guilders was still needed - a mere fraction of the total, but it was beyond us. If we didn't meet the terms of the contract, we would lose everything.

As the day drew nearer, I went to the other members of the community, urging them to pray. We had tried everything else; we just had to trust our way to God again. Many folk just could not believe that things would work out. They felt that we had taken on too much and that we were about to fall heavily, so it was a painful period of division. It wasn't the first time God left us waiting until almost the last moment - nor has it been the last - but it was certainly one of our most exciting moments of answered prayer when literally the day before the money was due, one of the girls in the Heidebeek family received a telegram from her father in America. He explained that he had recently sold a property, and God had told him to take the tithe from the proceeds and give it to us.

The money met the balance we owed with just 40 guilders over! There was great rejoicing that day as I ran around the property with telegram in hand, sharing the good news.

One summer's day not long after moving into Heidebeek, Sally and I were taking a walk in the countryside less than a mile from our buildings, when we came across a large house set back in the woods. We had never seen it before, but I was drawn towards the property strongly.

"Sally, there's something about that place," I told her. "Let's just pray about it right now."

As we stood in the country lane and bowed our heads, God put it on my heart to claim that house for Him. We looked up at the building once more before continuing our stroll.

Some weeks later an elderly lady came to see us. She introduced herself as a widow who lived in the very house we had been interested in. We were astounded as she told us her story.

"Twelve years ago my husband - he was a minister in the Reformed Church - and I came to live here. He felt God was telling him to start a training centre where young people could be equipped to serve the Lord in world evangelism. He died, and our dream never came to pass...."

We talked a while, and then she declared that she

wanted to give us the property - which turned out to be
not only the large house we had seen, but four more
smaller houses tucked away in the woods behind. These
properties, Herdershof - or The Shepherd's Fold - turned
out to be worth more than Heidebeek! It had been ours for
less than nine weeks when the first group of fifty students
moved in! Again, God's provision and timing had been
perfect.

It didn't end there, though. We held Sunday evening
meetings in the main hall at Heidebeek, and these soon
became so popular that not everyone could get in! Many
people had to listen to what was happening from the
corridors and side rooms. Not long after we prayed for
help to meet this problem, the owner of an old commercial
laundry a few hundred yards away came to us and said
that he wanted to sell the building, and the house that
went with it, to us. Once more the necessary money
seemed to come out of nowhere. While we were getting
the place ready, help came just when we needed it - free
sand and cement from a friend, cut-price carpeting -
always the right help at the right time! Soon between three
hundred and four hundred people were meeting each
week for praise, worship and teaching.

Another addition to the Heidebeek properties was in
1981, when Romkje - now married to Jeff Fountain, and
jointly leading the work at the training centre - was able to
take on a former old folks' home nearby, with a further
sixty-six rooms.

Since Heidebeek was established, well over one
thousand young people have attended the "spiritual boot
camp" to prepare and equip them for mission fields
around the world. The Discipleship Training Course is a
six month foundation course which is open to anyone
sensing God's call to service. There people learn about
studying the Bible, listening to God, spiritual warfare,
building relationships and evangelism. There is also the

opportunity to put all the classroom material to the test in short-term mission work across Europe, Africa and as far away as Asia. The places God has taken students to after finishing this course have not always been easy; but He never asks more of them than they can, with His Spirit, achieve.

Throughout Europe, the Americas and the Third World there are now Christians putting into practice all they have learnt through coming to the Centre to discover more about their God. Perhaps the strangest setting of all, though, is in a Northern Ireland prison.

"You ought to know, Floyd...." Patrick was obviously nervous, and took a deep breath before continuing. "I've been involved in murder...."

In the years that I had been working with new and young Christians, I had heard many heartbreaking stories of sad and sordid pasts, witnessed and shared many tears at hurts and wounds, and talked through the need for putting the past right. But this was the first time I had ever been confronted with someone who confessed to having blood on his hands. I was rocked.

Patrick had become a Christian through the combined efforts of YWAM and the Christian Youth Hostel in Amsterdam. We had a good working relationship with the people who ran the centre, and Patrick, like many others who were converted through the hostel, came on to The Ark for further discipling. He had been there for several months before going on to join the student community at Heidebeek for further training. Although still uncertain about what he should do, and cautious about whom he spoke to for fear that they might over-react in some way, Patrick poured out his story to me.

He had arrived in Amsterdam because he was on the run from the I.R.A., whose brutal campaign to free Northern Ireland from British rule he felt he could no longer support. He was also being sought by the Irish police, because his rejection of terrorism had not come about until he had been involved as an accomplice in three murders, and a number of other under-cover operations.

Patrick had hoped that as just another face in the large, drifting youth population of Amsterdam, his pursuers would forget about him in time. In the same way he hoped to forget his past, but that was before Jesus broke into his life, and began to insist that the complete forgiveness He had granted Patrick through His death on the cross be fleshed out in the young man's life.

"What happened - how were you involved?" I asked, still feeling stunned.

"I drove the car and acted as look-out when three men were assassinated." Patrick paused, then added "...murdered." He gave me some details, then looked at me. "What should I do?" he asked.

We prayed together: "Dear God, please guide us. We know you've forgiven Patrick - but where do we go from here? It's such a complicated situation, please help us to know the right thing."

We didn't come to any hasty conclusions that day, but we did talk long and hard about restitution and the need to put right, as far as possible, the mistakes we have made and the sins we've committed, as well as the need to seek forgiveness from those we have wronged. Things in the past need to be sorted out, as far as is practical, before we can go on. Jesus' death on the cross atoned for all our sins, but I believe that there are some things in our past life that we have to uncover before Him before they can be covered by His blood.

I thanked Patrick for his honesty with me and for his determination to do business with God. He knew where confronting this thing could lead.

I asked Patrick whether he felt those terrorist crimes

were dealt with as far as he was concerned, and whether he felt that he could return to his own country.

It was easier to ask the question than to answer it. It was one that we returned to in times of private discussion and prayer over the next few months, as Patrick moved on from Heidebeek's training school to help with our work in Amsterdam. He was seriously considering full-time service but I called him back, three or four times, to the question of his past.

"It's got to be your decision before God, Patrick, you know that. No-one can make it for you. But you have to come to know one way or the other how to deal with this thing, because you won't be free to go on until you have," I told him.

Finally he decided that he must return to meet the charges awaiting him. We knew the costliness of his choice, but felt that he was doing the right thing. Patrick flew back to Northern Ireland and, after several days' struggling with the finality of his decision, boldly marched into a Belfast police station and gave himself up.

The story of his conversion and resulting decision to surrender made newspaper headlines around the world when Patrick was subsequently sentenced to prison for life for his part as look-out and driver in the murder.

He is now serving his sentence in a bleak, special wing of one of Belfast's grey and formidable prisons - separated for his own protection from the rest of the prison population. He continues to honour God and witness commandingly for Him by his quiet, calm acceptance of his situation. Visiting him only recently, I was struck again, as I am each time, by the dramatic contrast of our meeting place. The oppressive, restrictive atmosphere of prison is a world away from the busy streets of Amsterdam where Patrick's self-determined walk to jail began.

Through the steadfastness of his faith in such difficult

and potentially depressing circumstances, I am convinced of the deep work of preparation God was doing in Patrick's life in those months before he finally decided to give himself up.

At the same time back in Amsterdam, preparation was also going on in John Goodfellow's life which would profoundly affect not just me but our work as a whole.

Eighteen

To the Streets!

Deep sobs punctuated the earnest prayer breaking the night's silence. My regular before-bed patrol of the teaching block at Heidebeek was interrupted by this unexpected encounter. Someone had let himself in to one of the classrooms to find a quiet place to be alone with God. I tip-toed to the door, not wanting to disturb his intimate communion, and strained to hear.

"Oh Father, please...please...the people out there are so lost, so blind. They need you so much. Please...change his heart, Father. Change his mind. Release us to go and tell those people how much You love them...please, Father...please..."

I was deeply moved by the heartbreak evident in the low voice - which I recognised as that of dear John Goodfellow. Then I realised that he was praying for me! My initial sense of empathy gave way to a cold wave of indignation, but as I crept away silently so as not to intrude on John's prayer-time, I recognised an increasingly familiar challenge being brought home. One that would not go away.

John was now part of the staff at the Discipleship Training School we were running. How he came to be back with us after returning home to Nottingham was another chapter in the remarkable story God was writing in this man's life. It had been three years earlier that he had headed for the sea ferry with an already well-thumbed Bible taking pride of place in his luggage. As arranged, police were waiting for him at the Harwich terminal, and he and his partners in crime - who had also decided to return and face the music - were whisked away in the back of a patrol car. Police confusion at their bizarre action in giving themselves up was compounded during the hours of interviews and waiting around in cells while prosecution files were completed. They calmly spent their spare time reading the Bible and, whenever the opportunity arose, spoke enthusiastically about their reasons for giving themselves up.

Released on bail, John was allowed to return home to his family. His solicitor had told him that the prospects looked very bleak. John had been charged with conspiracy to defraud - a very serious crime, which would almost certainly mean a jail sentence of several years.

"And this is probably the most clear-cut case of conspiracy I have ever dealt with - because you've told the police everything that happened," added John's counsel.

The previous conviction for the clumsy smash-and-grab raid was only bound to make matters worse, as well.

When John finally went on trial at Nottingham Crown Court, he told the story of his past and then without sentimentality explained about his conversion and the subsequent change in his life.

"I wouldn't be here in Court now if I hadn't become a Christian, because I wouldn't have given myself up. Being a Christian has changed my life and my values. I don't want to defraud people now, but I want to share what I've found and help others."

The frankly-told story seemed to impress the judge and he gave John and his friends suspended sentences. It was a miraculous decision, even with the letters and character references we had supplied from Amsterdam, vouching for their reform. Neither John nor his friends could believe that they were free to walk away from the courtroom.

John celebrated his unexpected freedom by going home and making a list of all the people he could remember having stolen from or wronged in some way. With a criminal past dating back ten years, it was a long list and he worked out that he owed several thousand pounds. The following morning, after an early period of prayer and Bible-reading, he put on his best suit and set out to visit everyone on the list that he could.

It was a long day, and there were many surprised faces in the banks, shops and offices that John visited. He introduced himself, told about his conversion and court appearance, and then admitted he had stolen or defrauded money from them. He went on to explain that he wanted to pay it back.

There were mixed reactions - some demanded payment immediately, while others were so astonished to hear his story that they just thanked him for his honesty and cancelled the debt there and then. In the evening John wrote to everyone he had been unable to visit, setting out his apology and determination to repay them in similar style.

John, who then lived at home with his family, soon found himself work as a bricklayer, and with his first pay packet went out and bought a little black directory. Into it went all the names and addresses of the people to whom he owed money. Then began what was to become a weekly ritual over the next two-and-a-half-years; he went to the Post Office, bought postal orders, filled them in and despatched them to the string of addresses. Keeping just a few pounds to pay for his keep, travel, and the occasional cup of coffee, John remained punctual in his payments and regular in his employment throughout the following months.

This new-found integrity made its mark in the home.

The family, used to a very different John, were at first suspicious - was this another "con"? Then they were curious, and finally, one-by-one, won over by the same love that had first spoken to John. First his two sisters, then his mother, and finally his father give their lives to Christ through John's radiant witness. Those months together were a sweet time of forgiveness and reconciliation in a home that had known much hurt and division. They were particularly special for John, because his father died in a tragic road accident just a few months after his conversion.

We were following these wonderful events through the regular letters John sent back to The Ark. Eventually we felt we had to send over workers from Amsterdam - Paul and Mary Miller - to help disciple and nurture all those who had become Christians through their contact with John. With a zealous heart he wanted to share what he had found with his old friends - scouring the old haunts of pubs and clubs to meet up with them and tell them how his life had been turned around. Then he turned his attention to the streets, where his own first visible contact for Christ had occurred.

Each Saturday he went down into Nottingham's shopping area - sometimes joined by one of his sisters and another friend - and preached at the top of his voice about the love of God which had dramatically changed his life. Though he was still only a Christian of nine months, God had already built strong spiritual foundations into his life, for John was soon leading a group of about sixty people who had come to the Lord through his witnessing in the open air and through personal contact with him.

Paul and Mary arrived to help him establish a permanent YWAM ministry in Nottingham and to build on all that God had begun to do. John told them excitedly about the overwhelming compulsion he had to go out into the streets to tell people about Jesus, and the remarkable way he had seen God move.

"I'd travelled all over Europe, but I never met an on-fire, witnessing Christian until I was twenty-six. It wasn't until then that anyone told me that Jesus Christ loved me and died to set me free," he explained as his motivation. "The first time I heard the gospel I loved it, wanted it, craved it. I accepted all that God had done for me. Just think how many other people there must be like me out there, who have never really heard about Him..."

Some months later John came back to Holland to visit one of his sisters, who was going through the Discipleship Training School at Heidebeek. He had intended to stay just a few days, but stayed on and completed his own D.T.S. His plan had been to return home to continue paying off the huge debts which he was about halfway through clearing. I felt that he would be a tremendous asset to the YWAM work and invited him to stay on as a staff member. I threw down a challenge - why didn't he ask God for a sign whether or not he should stay on? Why not ask for some divine help in clearing the rest of the debts, if that was what was keeping him from joining us? John readily agreed to this secret, unadvertised agreement we struck with God. And over the next few weeks money poured in from nowhere to clear his little black book of debts. In the mornings John went to his pigeonhole and there would be another envelope, containing an anonymous or unsolicited gift. It was miraculous provision, and convinced us both that John should stay on in Holland.

It was then that the tables were turned, and John called me gradually to a point of decision. We knew all about the remarkable work God had been doing through him in Nottingham, and of his exploits preaching on the streets. This desire to talk in public about God's salvation was something that he couldn't explain even to himself. Soon he began coming to me to ask whether I would allow him to take a small team out onto the streets in Amsterdam for some open air preaching.

I refused point blank. Such aggressive, even confrontational, methods of evangelism were not what we had pioneered and developed over the years in our work in friendship evangelism. It simply wasn't right for the kind of situation we were dealing with, it was too crude and uncaring. I told him it didn't and wouldn't work. Graciously John accepted my decision and went away - only to come back a couple of weeks later to repeat his request.

This game of request and refusal had been going on for several months the night I stumbled over his tearful prayers. His sincerity and deep concern for the people he wanted to tell about Jesus really made its mark. They confirmed the nagging doubts about my stand that had been growing over the course of our discussions on the issue. I didn't give way right then because I recognised that many of the suspicions and even, to a degree, the cynicism I had harboured about such kinds of evangelism would have to be faced and dealt with. John's fortnightly pleas continued. Then, one day, he asked again in his courteous way.

"OK, John. Go ahead. Give it a try," I told him after taking a deep breath.

"Pardon?"

"I said, 'OK'. Try it. Let's see what happens. But I'm allowing you to go on two conditions."

"All right," John beamed. He would have accepted them if he'd had to stand on his head and paint his feet pink, he was so delighted. "What are they, Floyd?"

"Don't yell or scream at anybody," I cautioned. "And don't talk about hell!" I was concerned about identifying ourselves with a "turn or burn" approach to evangelism.

So it was a few days later that John set off for Amsterdam with a team from Heidebeek. Some of the girls had practised some Israeli-style folk dances, and created colourful costumes. Setting down a tape machine in the centre of Dam Square - Amsterdam's crossroads for junkies, tourists and shoppers - they launched into an impromptu display. They scattered the pigeons, but drew a delighted crowd of several hundred people.

Standing to observe a little way off, I was astonished by the favourable reaction - even when the dancing finished and John stepped up to speak briefly about why they were so happy. He explained the difference Jesus made in their lives and why they wanted to share their joy with others.

That first, simple exercise in public proclamation was something of a watershed. I had been brought face-to-face with all my unreasonable prejudices, and seen them exposed for what they were. Convictions mixed with a dash of insecurity had resulted in an unyielding denial that anything worthwhile could come from such forms of public evangelism. To this day I hold that such approaches can be misused and abused with the damaging results we found evidence of in our work among the Afghan drop-outs, but that afternoon in Amsterdam I saw a whole new avenue opening up before us. I was reminded of two incidents which had occurred soon after our arrival in Holland from the East.

Keen to get a bearing on Amsterdam, I had begun to walk its streets almost within hours of dumping our possessions on The Ark. The city was flooded with hippies and drop-outs from all over Europe as it celebrated the height of flower power popularity. I toured their hostels and haunts, visiting famous - or, rather, infamous - nightclubs like *The Milky Way*, and *The Paradiso*, to try to gauge the pulse of the environment. I quickly became overwhelmed with the sense that beyond The Ark's bows there was an entire city that God wanted to reach. Not just a sector of the community like the needy young people we had been working with in Kabul - but an entire population. Beyond the counter-culture, I saw the rest of the community needing Jesus - students, drug addicts, prostitutes, ethnic minorities, tourists, businessmen, housewives, children. A whole city, whole groups of people. "Some day," I had sensed the Spirit telling me, "I want you to reach the whole city. I'll tell you when."

The other incident which confirmed this was when Romkje Fountain introduced us to Tante Corrie - Corrie Ten Boom.

We had known rejection from some corners of the Church for our "Jesus People" image, but if Tante Corrie ever even noticed that we didn't look like the average Sunday churchgoer, she never let on. She just loved us, supported us and encouraged us from our first meeting. On several occasions, she came down to speak at our Sunday evening meetings on The Ark. The stories she told of her family's suffering at the hands of the Nazis, her struggles with bitterness and forgiveness through her days in the concentration camp, made a deep impact on our young people, many of whom were struggling with their own feelings of alienation and rejection. Shared experiences bridged the years. She became a grandmother to us all. On one occasion when she had been invited over to America on a major speaking tour, shortly before departure she came to us and asked us to lay hands on her, to pray and "send her out". We were honoured and humbled that such a saintly old lady, internationally respected for her ministry, should come to us in this way. And we were tickled by the thought that this slight spinster in her seventies was "our" missionary!

One weekend Tante Corrie invited Sally and me to take the children to her little home in Haarlem, just a few miles away from The Ark, to get away from the pressure of the houseboats for a while. I decided to take advantage of the spiritual environment we were in by praying late into the

night. It was during that prayer-time that I was impressed
by the burden to reach beyond the drop-outs and the
"freaks" to Amsterdam as a whole. Impressions, no more
than seed thoughts, of new and exciting ways of
evangelising different parts of the city came to me, and I
sensed that one day music, drama and cross cultural
missions would be an integral part of our outreach in the
city.

These feelings, half-forgotten, were brought sharply
back into focus as I watched John's joyful troupe on the
Dam Square. For the first time I saw clearly that public
evangelism of this kind could be complementary to what
we had worked so hard towards in friendship evangelism.
The two didn't have to be in conflict. I saw that such
initiatives had the potential to bring us into contact with
many people for whom our friendship evangelism
approach would not be enough to gain us entrance into
their lives. I became excited, thanked John for his patient
love and persistence with me - and asked God to forgive
me for all the wrong attitudes I had harboured for so long.

Soon teams were driving into the city almost every
weekend, with music and dance being used to attract a
large crowd before a short gospel message was presented.
One day John jokingly asked me when I was going to have
a turn at speaking. I passed it off with a light comment,
but inside I realised that I was actually a little fearful of
standing up in the open to preach in that way.

This vulnerability began to bother me, but I knew I had
to face it. In my early days with YWAM in America and
Great Britain, I had often spoken at university and college
campuses on apologetics, showing the historical logical
basis of Christianity. I began to look for illustrations and
material that could be adapted for the demands of short,
thought-provoking street preaching. One Saturday after
the crowd-pulling drama, I stepped up to speak, my heart
thumping hard. To my surprise, I found that I loved it,

and was stimulated by the different reactions of the crowd. I sensed, as I looked at them, some of God's longing for them to come to know Him.

Our weekly forays from Heidebeek created some tensions with members of The Ark community, though. I had preached friendship evangelism so long and so hard that my new commitment to public proclamation of the gospel was hard for them to accept and understand. I had always maintained that friendship evangelism was about people as individuals having worth and meaning. How did this fit in now with standing on a street corner and raising my voice, shouting at people? It seemed as if I was denying all I had ever stood so firmly for. I sympathised with their misgivings, because it had taken me some time to work through this myself. For a while there was a real sense of divorce between the two approaches to evangelism for several of The Ark team. Gradually, though, they came round as I had, and saw the new dimension that John Goodfellow was leading us into as an exciting expansion, not a denial, of all that we knew.

Not everyone wanted to be our friends, but they still needed to know about Jesus. Public proclamation might be the only opportunity we had to tell them about Him. And it was clear even from early responses that there were passers-by who heard the gospel for whom the timing was just right. Our vision had broadened.

We approached the open air work as another way of drawing people into our existing pattern of friendship, discipleship and nurture. The idea was to go out into the streets, attract people's attention with a short message, and then break off into the crowd to follow up with one-to-one conversations. Anyone showing a keen interest would be invited back for coffee and further dialogue. Amsterdam had traditionally been a venue for colourful street performers - the old barrel organs competing with impromptu rock concerts and other performing arts - so our presentations had to have more impact then would come from simply standing up on a box and talking. We began to pour hours of creative thinking and prayer into devising short dramas, music and other events to gain people's attention. We endeavoured to communicate effectively about issues and pressures related to everyday life.

Among our earliest, unlikely, partners in proclaiming the gospel around Amsterdam's streets was a gang of Hell's Angels.

The volunteers who joined us in the city for our first summer campaigns had to make do with somewhat primitive conditions at a camp-site on the outskirts of the city. They threw themselves into the programme with enthusiasm, spending part of each day in prayer and praise before heading out onto the streets. One Sunday afternoon, a few members of one group were taking a break in Vondel Park, enjoying their sandwiches in the sun, when a gang of bikers lounging around nearby began to let it be known in loud, aggressive and clear-cut terms that they could do without the likes of these "Jesus freaks" crowding them out.

It was a menacing atmosphere, and it looked for a time as though their verbal abuse might easily spill over into physical violence. Sensing the unrest, some of the YWAM youngsters went over to talk to the bikers, and invited them to join the picnic. This defused the situation almost immediately, and pretty soon the two groups - the fresh-faced young missionaries, and the greasy, leather-clad Hell's Angels - were sitting together almost like old friends! As if to return the compliment, the bikers invited the team back to their clubhouse.

This was an offer too good to refuse, but as John Goodfellow, who was leading the team, recalled, it was an eye-opening experience.

"What we saw inside this dirty, rundown old building was just unbelievable. There were about thirty-five kids in there, with heroin syringes all over the place. Some guys were fighting - there was even somebody tearing around in there on a motorbike! The people who had invited us there protected us from the others! The most amazing thing though was that they had taken us along there to preach the gospel to their 'mates'!"

It wasn't long before a firm friendship developed between the two groups, and whenever any street evangelism was being attempted there were always a few gang members hanging around quietly in the background to make sure that there was no trouble. Though their threats to hecklers of "Shut up, or we'll smash your face in!" were not exactly consistent with the message of love that was being delivered, we appreciated their protection! It was amazing how respectful people were to us when our "Guardian Angels" were around!

It was also surprising to witness the response that open air evangelism could provoke from passers-by. Maybe it had something to do with Amsterdam's tradition of free-speech and tolerance, but we soon found that there were some ways of going about street preaching that were going to be less successful than others. My initial ban on talking about hell wasn't an attempt to soft-pedal the gospel, but based on an awareness of how often fire-and-brimstone addresses of that kind presented in a vacuum, with no foundation of personal commitment to the people and the community, simply got people's backs up. They either just heckled or didn't even stop to listen. So we attempted to present the truth: that man's sin has cut him off from God, and only through repentance and faith in Christ's death on the cross can we be restored to a relationship with Him. We wanted a reaction from the people who stopped to hear us. We wanted them to talk, to respond and to reason. We knew that declaring God's

Word would bring conviction and even anger, but we wanted to make sure that people stayed around long enough to hear what we had to say. We wanted them to listen and then challenge us on it, rather than just dismiss us as self-righteous, condemnatory Bible-bashers.

Even so we made mistakes. We found, for instance, that preaching publicly against homosexuality produced an entirely negative reaction. In a city famous for its historical commitment to harbour and protect those persecuted in society, our denouncing of homosexuality violated the Amsterdammers' commitment to protect the underdog. We were violating the ordinary man's sense of right and wrong. As part of its sexual liberation - and believe me this is carried to gross extremes in Amsterdam, which is recognised as the gay capital of Europe - there is even a monument to gay life in one of the city squares. An estimated ten to fifty thousand gay men and women arrive in the city each weekend for its celebrated nightlife and gay scene. Even heterosexual people, including grandmothers, reacted aggressively when we spoke out against homosexual practices and pointed to such activity in the city as one indication of how far Amsterdam had strayed from God's standards.

We talked and prayed about a new approach towards the homosexual community and now prefer to concentrate on personal evangelism among them. Several of our workers are committed full-time to witnessing to, counselling and caring for members of the city's large gay population. We firmly believe that God views homosexual relationships as sin, but we could also see that focusing on it in our street preaching was having a completely unhelpful effect. Homosexuality is no more or less a sin than stealing or lying, as far as the Bible is concerned. Many homosexuals, who experienced years of prejudice from society and the Church, could only see us as being judgmental towards them. They could not see that we separated the sin from the sinner.

Ironically our views exposed us to prejudice in this city famous for its tolerance! On occasions when we have been asked our views towards homosexuality and have spelled out where we stand Biblically, we have been refused permission to book halls and other premises for meetings and conferences, because we are "anti-gay".

As time went on, we began to realise that even with The Ark and our new developing street work, we weren't really getting to grips with some of the problems and challenges of the city, particularly in the Red Light quarter. We recognised that even the most well-organised and presented public presentation of the gospel was not going to be enough on its own. It wasn't enough to engage in guerilla type tactics - going in to preach and witness, then retreating to our base to return for conversations with anyone who showed interest.

We needed to take our twin thrust of bold proclamation and firm friendship right to the Devil's doorstep; into the diseased heart of Amsterdam's grey world of sex, drugs and the occult.

During 1978, as our street work became increasingly established and effective, I began to sense that God was telling me our family would be moving back into the city as part of this new initiative. I was delighted because in spite of all the joys of family living at Heidebeek, with its bubbling streams and idyllic peacefulness, I sorely missed the challenge of being in the city.

Practically, though, raising a family in the city would be a different prospect to when we had left. Then our two children had been little more than babies, vulnerable mostly to the physical dangers of life in such a bustling, brusque environment. Now they were growing, curious young children of six and four years old - open to all the potential dangers of being harmed emotionally and spiritually by the city's twisted character. Aspects that in the past would have been over their heads could now go straight to their hearts. It was a very big step and one not to be taken lightly.

Sally had thrown all her creativity into making our first home a special place at Heidebeek. She had loved fashioning and shaping our rooms over the last few years. We had saved the biggest project until the last and Sally had just finished creating a farm-style kitchen which was her pride and joy. Our home was restful and had a character all of its own. We felt secure and although I wanted to go back into the busy life of the city, the tranquillity at Heidebeek would be sorely missed.

I knew I had to say something to Sally so, after a visit to Amsterdam one day, I went into the kitchen and said:

"Sally, can we sit down? I want to share something with you - it's really important."

We sat down together at the kitchen table and Sally looked enquiringly at me. I continued:

"Now I don't expect an answer to this right away. Just think about what I'm going to say, and pray, and then you can respond."

I looked around and was really worried about what I had to say because I knew how much the kitchen meant to Sally.

"I've been praying about this for a long time and I feel the Lord wants us to move back to Amsterdam. I'd like you to pray about it."

Although Sally did not look surprised, she started to cry.

"Where would we live? What would we do?" she asked.

"I feel a burden for Amsterdam and think it's right to live in the heart of the city."

Sally looked questioningly.

"In the Red Light District."

Sally began to cry. "Oh Floyd."

"Look, let's think and pray about it." We had a long discussion and I told her that I wouldn't bring up the subject again until she had prayed about it and thought it through.

She nodded in quiet agreement, we prayed and then left it.

One day, three months later, she broke the silence.

"When I cried about moving into the city, you know it wasn't because I didn't want to go - it was the idea of taking our children into the Red Light District that upset me. I had felt that we would be returning to Amsterdam when we left The Ark - but I wasn't expecting to go there. I've worked it through with God now, Floyd," she added. "I've come to a sense of peace, and I know the Lord will help us work through the problems. I feel it's right and I've resolved my fears and tensions."

Our independent and joint convictions that God was calling us right into the heart of the city were to be tested hard. It was probably just as well that we didn't know then quite how hard.

Nineteen

Scared in the City

The two faces of Amsterdam's popular tourist trade stare at each other across a narrow street on one of the city's many picturesque tree-lined waterways.

The massive greying Oude Kerk, or Old Church, is the oldest and biggest church building in the city and was consecrated over six hundred years ago. With its magnificent Gothic stone carvings and impressive stained glass windows, it represents beauty and culture and attracts a steady stream of visitors. It is also the venue for many of the city's pipe organ concerts. Unfortunately on all sides of the huge church walls there are old three or four storey houses in which prostitutes live and work, and these attract another type of visitor.

The girls, sitting or standing, some smoking, chewing gum, filing their nails or just looking vacantly into the street, wait like livestock at a cattle market for the next buyer.

Amsterdam's Red Light District is an integral part of the city's tourist scene. It is advertised in many of the travel brochures which champion its adult, broad-minded and tolerant approach to nightlife. The streets and alleys are included in the itinerary of many walking tours or boat rides of the city.

"That is Anne Frank's house, where she wrote her famous diary while in hiding during World War Two," explain the guides. "Look up at all the different gables, for which Amsterdam's houses are famous ... see the hippy barges...look at the many bicycles there are everywhere ....and over there are the girls in their windows...."

Amsterdam's Red Light District is famous the world over for its boldness. The prostitutes sit in the windows of their small rooms, wearing little or nothing, for the passers-by to stare at. It is a curious tradition that has developed over the years. Like all seafaring cities, Amsterdam has long had its prostitutes catering for the ships that come in. Probably it was the competition that forced the girls to become more blatant in their advertising. First the traditional lights in the windows, then moving out onto the streets to solicit openly, finally setting themselves up in vulgar shop windows. It must have been an indication of its international renown that, a couple of years ago, Amsterdam was selected as the venue for a world-wide gathering of prostitutes to discuss the way changes in the law could affect their business.

We had known for some time that we needed a permanent physical presence in the neighbourhood, and prayed long and hard, when Peter Fitzgerald and John Goodfellow came upon the Budget Hotel. Squeezed in between a Satanist church and a sex cinema on what was possibly the district's most notorious thoroughfare, it was a cramped, rundown old hostel that had been used as a student boarding house, and was lying vacant in a considerable state of disrepair when we found it in early 1979. It was here that we found the place that was to be our first foothold in the Red Light District.

Negotiations for the purchase of the property weren't made any easier by the fact that the owner was evading the police over a little matter of unpaid taxes. We had to meet him clandestinely to discuss terms, but he turned down our offer of 175,000 guilders without even drawing breath. The meeting was over almost before we had realised, and all our prayers and plans seemed to have been in vain.

John, Peter and I walked round to a small chapel, named after its address, "O.Z. 100", on one of the district's other busy streets. It is run by a small Christian community, and the sunken, stone-floored little chapel made a wonderfully peaceful retreat from the aggressive environment just outside. A small waterfall trickled down into a man-sized basin at one end of the chapel. The cool and calm of the place often drew our workers for a few moments' stillness away from the hurly-burly of the streets. It was there that we took our disappointment and confusion to God.

As we prayed together, we sensed that we should raise our offer to 230,000 guilders - a compromise between our original offer and the asking price. We felt this was God's leading, so we prayed for confirmation. If this was right, we asked the Lord to confirm it by leading us to the elusive owner somewhere on the streets as we walked back to The Ark, so that the sale could go through quickly.

We prayed as we left the chapel and as we wound our way through the busy streets the impossible happened. We walked straight into the owner we had met only a few minutes previously!

We stopped him and made our new bid. "It's a deal," he said and with tourists and "pushers" passing by on either side, we finalised the agreement to take over the former hotel.

Wedged between larger buildings and with its rabbit warren of rooms, any passers-by would think that the new name we gave it, "The Cleft", was singularly appropriate. It seemed to have been jammed into place, rather than built. It looks, as the name suggests, little more than a fissure in the rock. There is however a great significance to the renaming. "The Cleft" is as deep into "enemy territory" as it is possible to go, right at the core of the Red

Light District. To us it symbolises the rock in the wilderness which Moses struck with his rod, and from which God caused water to come streaming out. It was our prayer, as we dedicated the building to its new role, that He would use it in the same way, pouring new life into all those in the surrounding desert of immorality.

When the paperwork had been completed, John Goodfellow took a volunteer crew of forty-five young people into the building for a month's renovation blitz. They rebuilt and repaired from top to bottom, and constructed an ingenious system of three-tier bunk beds. This meant that by summer time the tiny hotel could accommodate around fifty people, in relative comfort, for a short term outreach programme.

Even this didn't fulfil our purpose for the building, though. We knew that we had to establish a permanent presence there. The people we wanted to reach had to stop being objects of our outreaches, and start being our neighbours. So we decided to open a small cafe in what had been the pool hall and drinking area downstairs. After much discussion and prayer, John and Jan Kennedy, two of the leaders from Heidebeek, moved in with their two children and a small team of helpers to establish the work there. John and Jan were happy to do this on a temporary basis, but were not sure how long they would stay.

It was a year before Sally and I moved into the top floor flat at "The Cleft" with Misha and Matthew. By this time we had had discussions with John and Jan, who were now thinking in terms of a more permanent ministry at "The Cleft". They had discovered many of the practical problems of living in such an area, particularly with young children.

Many close friends and supporters expressed surprise - some, concern - over our suggested move into the neighbourhood. How could we even consider such a thing with small children? As we talked and prayed about it over many evenings, Sally and I began to see clearly just how - and why.

Over the years we had been in Holland, God had been equipping and establishing YWAM as a ministry. In the past we might not have been spiritually mature or experienced enough to take on the challenge of living and ministering in the Red Light District. In our early days on The Ark we had largely avoided the area, warning our workers against the dangers of going there out of curiosity. We knew that we could only move into such situations in God's authority. We had seen other works started up without proper preparation. The resulting breakdowns of ministries and individuals had been distressing to witness.

But now we sensed as a YWAM team that God was calling us to make such a move. God wanted us to spread His love in the Red Light District, and He didn't want us to see the hurting, needy people there as "problems" to work with, but people to live among. He wanted us to see them, not as prostitutes, pimps and pushers, but as people lovingly created in His image.

Jesus had walked this earth because He loved people like Mary Magdalene, the lepers and Pharisees, just as much as He did those who were to become His closest friends and followers. He longed to be allowed into their lives with His freedom-giving gentleness and grace - that was why He was calling us to this grim part of Amsterdam.

It was not a decision to take lightly. Of course there would be problems, even a degree of risk, but it was not irresponsible if God had called us. We could not be safer or more secure than in the place where God wanted us to be. Past experience had shown us that. Being a family though changed things. One friend brought us a comforting reassurance one day, when she told Sally:

"You know, God loves your children even more than you do. So that means He would never lead you into something that would in the long run be harmful to them".

Telling our parents of the decision was not easy. Although both my parents and Sally's had been concerned about our living in Afghanistan, they hadn't fully appreciated how bad it was - but everyone has an idea of what life in the Red Light District must be like.

My parents were both godly people, and having been pastors for over thirty years approached the problem from a prayerful angle rather than by natural instinct. Sally's mother, who was now widowed, was also a godly woman and once she had prayed about the situation, remembered an interesting fact - that just after she became a Christian she herself had gone to witness to prostitutes in her own home town, until she was told by her pastor that he thought it unwise. Sally's mom had longed to do this work and for many months afterwards kept on praying for these girls. She was therefore delighted to realise that a lot of what was in her heart was being fulfilled in what Sally and I were going to do. It brought a completely new perspective on the matter.

God was not just calling Sally and me to this work - He was calling us as a family, which meant the children as well, and as such He would look after us and protect us. We had to be prepared to act on the belief that our security was in God, not where we lived. If we followed Him in faith and humility, trusting Him for all that we needed, then we felt that we would be bequeathing a spiritual legacy to our children which would mean far more than any amount of money or material happiness. We believed that there were more pitfalls and dangers facing those living in the apparent safety and serenity of suburbia, with one eye on the mortgage and the other on the video recorder.

There are Christians living in such neighbourhoods because they know that they have been called there to be salt and light, so it is God's sovereign lordship in their lives which keeps them there. But there are many people who are living in comfort because they simply want to be there. Despite all we have experienced since moving into the Red Light District, we still believe that these families face greater danger than we do. In fact, we believe one of the reasons God called us to live in the heart of the city was to challenge other families about their values and direction in life. God wants to use every family in some form of ministry, and that only comes as parents seek God for His purposes for their family collectively.

The mugger, the porn industry and drug pushers are recognisable threats. The lure of materialism and its spirit-sapping insidiousness is far harder to identify, but it can be equally devastating in its effect on a family. You can't get much further from God than a life in which you, and not He, are number one. Some people get their kicks from handing over money - for drugs, sex, or whatever. Others get theirs by making money and hoarding it. Each is a form of addiction to what they perceive as personal happiness, whether it is a drug-blown oblivion, or designer-style living.

We involved our children in the process of decision-making. After all, they were going to be an integral part of what we were doing. Since they were infants we had encouraged them by teaching and example to develop an intimate and easy-going relationship with God. So now, facing this major decision, we asked them to pray about it too, and to let us know their feelings and thoughts.

Four year old Matthew came to us one day and announced simply that he had talked with Jesus about it and he felt OK. Some time later Sally, Misha and I were driving in the car.

"Have you prayed about moving to Amsterdam,

Misha?" Sally asked.

"No. Can I pray now and have your Bible, please?"

"Sure," said Sally as she passed it over. Misha took such a long time leafing through the Bible and praying that Sally and I looked at each other wondering what was going to happen. We were slightly amused but also pleased that she was taking it so seriously.

"Mommy, where is that song we sing - 'He has shown you oh man what is good'?" We recognised it was from Micah chapter six verse eight and showed it to Misha who looked at it quietly for some minutes, then went through it phrase by phrase.

"'He has shown you, oh man, what is good' - that means Mommy and Daddy that he has shown you what to do. 'What does the Lord require of you?' - He requires us to move to Amsterdam. 'To act justly and to love mercy' - He wants to help the prostitutes find Jesus and mercy. 'To walk humbly with your God' - that's what He wants us to do as a family."

Sally and I just looked at each other. We were amazed at the maturity Misha had shown and were so thankful to the Lord for it. Many times we thought back to this conversation when we first moved into Amsterdam's Red Light District. We had come to the point as a family where we were certain that this was what God wanted us to do, and it was a conviction which we had to hold onto many times over the years when we were tempted to believe that it was all a dreadful mistake.

Twenty

On the Devil's Doorstep

The switch from twenty-five acres of delightful countryside to three tiny rooms in a run-down apartment was just too great to make in a moment.

Instead we prepared gradually for the transfer over the better part of a year, helping Misha and Matthew make the transition slowly. Sally and I fixed up the little rooms to make them "home", and we then took the children into the city one day a week, to start getting them used to such a new environment. As our children were older than the Kennedys', we thought they needed more time to adjust, and this proved to be the case.

These trips usually took place during the day, but one time Sally found herself driving the youngsters through the streets near The Cleft after dark. Although the Red Light District is "in business" all day long, it really comes alive at night, when the neon signs cut through the darkness, and the bright lights make an immediate visual impact. Sally gradually realised that all had gone dreadfully quiet in the back of the car as the two children drank in all they saw. Then Matthew piped up, with a mixture of shock and indignation: "Mom, those ladies haven't got any clothes on! Why not?"

This needed a special measure of wisdom, and as Sally shot a quick prayer heavenwards, it came from an unexpected quarter.

"Well, that's what sin does to people," explained Misha simply. "We all have choices to make. When you're little, they don't seem to be very important, but if you make the wrong ones, when you get bigger you think the wrong choices are the right ones."

Sally could hardly believe what she was hearing, but once again was grateful for Misha's maturity and spiritual understanding.

Sally and I needed similar childlike insight frequently. When we were living at The Cleft full-time, the children's eyes were opened even more widely to the whole sexual nature of the environment. Because the Kennedys had already experienced living in this area, their advice was very helpful. Together we learnt a great deal about raising children in such an awkward situation. Many questions were asked, most of which you wouldn't expect to come from youngsters twice their age. They were being sensitised daily through what they saw in the streets, and through their contacts at their new school. Most of the pupils lived in the neighbourhood, and many of their parents ran sex clubs or bars - some even had mothers who worked in the windows.

Misha was the only pupil in her class of thirteen whose mother and father were still living together. One day Matthew came home from school and described a sex gadget that one of the young boys in his class had been wearing on his key-ring. His father had given it to him from his shop. "What's it for?" Matthew wondered.

These questions needed honest and careful answers. We wanted to be truthful but didn't want to give more information that they were able to understand. We wanted to nurture a positive, wholesome attitude to sex education. Time and again God came to our rescue, giving us insights and ways of sharing His truths when we just didn't know how to respond. In answer to their queries, we told the children that the women in the windows slept with other men, which the Bible said was wrong. It upset God, and hurt Him because they were not living with their husbands. What they were doing was bad, but God still loved them. Though we did not go into detail about the nature of people's sins, our children understood that when a person was married they should be loyal to their husband or wife. We learnt to allow the children's questions to guide us as to how much we told them. We only went into detail when it was necessary. We explained that God wanted a man and a woman to love each other. Later we told them about the nature of people's sexual sins and how these people were paying for sex and as a result, devaluing and spoiling it. We also said that the people who came round to look at the women were wrong.

There were times when we grieved that our children were exposed to such harsh realities so young, but we trusted God, and we saw that faith vindicated. Their experience has given Misha and Matthew a very real appreciation of just what sin does to people. They see beyond the thin, glamorous veil to the pain and hurt beneath. So much so that when some of Misha's friends at school talk about how they hope to go into the windows one day like their mothers and aunts, she is deeply troubled. Our children have a healthy understanding of the true nature of sin and its effects; being made aware of it so young has not affected them for ill.

Often the task of handling these curious enquiries - like much of the day-to-day burden of living out our everyday calling of being a family in the Red Light District - has fallen on Sally's shoulders. It was she who brought us an important perspective on our new home shortly after we moved our final belongings to The Cleft.

A few days after I deposited the last bags on the floor of our apartment, I had to leave for a fortnight's conference in Thailand. The day after I left, it began to rain - hard and long. Sally and the two children were cooped up inside the entire time, unable to venture out to a nearby park. Matthew began crying that first morning, sobbing that he wanted to go back and play with his friends at Heidebeek. He carried on crying for the next two weeks, and by the time I managed to 'phone home, Sally's tears had started too.

I felt torn in two - here I was halfway round the world unable to comfort them, and there they were suffering. Even Pooh, our faithful spaniel, was finding the adjustment difficult. Bereft of her beloved fields and trees, and overwhelmed by the noise, she had refused to eat or drink until Sally finally had to take her to the vet and eventually force-feed her.

When I got home, Sally told me how God had used those despairing early days to teach her an important lesson for our new home. We were all convinced as a family that God had called us to The Cleft, but if we weren't careful, Misha and Matthew could understandably develop a very negative view of God's will and purpose. To counter this, we set out to learn a real appreciation of all the good things in the city. We took one and sometimes two days a week to explore our new environment as a family, and enjoyed trips on the canals, visits to the fascinating museums and galleries and walks in the parks. Outings for mugs of hot chocolate and ice creams at the corner cafes and, of course, regular visits to McDonalds, were all popular. Misha and Sally went to the ballet, Matthew and I went down to the docks to watch the boats. We discovered all kinds of exciting things to do that were not available to us when living out in the quiet countryside.

In addition to this discovery, God showed me the need to find spiritual fulfilment in the city. The peacefulness of Heidebeek had been special, but God wanted us to see that He wasn't only present in Swiss-chalet style surroundings, but could be found, appreciated and enjoyed in the hustle and bustle, even the wickedness, of big cities. He loved the cities of the world, and wanted His children to start loving them too rather than turning their backs on them. My eyes were opened to this dimension through a series of meditations on the book of Jonah, which profoundly shaped my attitudes to the work we were pioneering.

Immoral, cruel, idolatrous, militaristic - Nineveh was all these things. God hated all these manifestations of evil, but He still loved the people there so much that He sent someone to tell them about Him. What did Jonah do? He headed for the suburbs - to the peace and quiet of Tarshish. He found though that he was safer and more fulfilled when he finally turned round and went where God wanted him - to the most wicked city of the day. I began to see the city more clearly through God's eyes, with some of His compassion and love.

Just after we moved into The Cleft, a Dutch Reformed minister welcomed us to the district with a bouquet of flowers. With tears in his eyes, he said, "You are an answer to prayer. My family have been living in the Red Light District for over twenty years and have been praying for more families to arrive. Thank you for coming." We were very touched by this.

Domestic changes took some getting used to, as well. All of Sally's gifts in adapting to new circumstances, and fashioning a home from very little, were called on. From a just-finished home at Heidebeek with its coveted kitchen, we had come to three small rooms, and a little corner kitchen that had to be shared with the twenty or so other people living at The Cleft. Our own living room was so small, that when I sat down in our easy chair and stretched my legs out, nobody else could get into the room without having to step over me!

The Lord is always just and fair and He doesn't take

away things which are meaningful and special without replacing them. We had lost the space and freedom of Heidebeek but in its place our family unit became much closer. We faced the difficulties together and this, to us, was much more important than the nice kitchen we had left.

Because it rains frequently in Amsterdam, and even on clear days mothers and children don't venture out into the Red Light District unescorted, Misha and Matthew had to develop new interests and activities. At first it was a real struggle for them, as they had been used to having plenty of space in which to burn up their boundless energy. Sally invested money and time in a range of stimulating educational toys, to encourage new hobbies and games. We prayed that the children wouldn't see their new lifestyle as a prison, but explore new areas of their personality. Misha's love for drawing grew, and she spent many hours at work on her sketch pad. Matthew loved to make up stories. He tried them out on Pooh - they would sit together in the corner - and Matthew would talk to him for hours. Later he began to write them down. Both drawing and writing are gifts that are still developing in Misha and Matthew.

The problems didn't go away quickly, but gradually over the course of six months we began to feel a genuine love for all we could enjoy because of living in the city. Now, when asked whether they would like to go back to the open-spaced freedom of Heidebeek, Matthew and Misha cry, "Oh no, we love living in the city."

While confinement replaced freedom, the peace and tranquillity of Heidebeek also gave way to noise and distractions. Four and five nights a week we would be awakened during the small hours by dreadful noises. The canals and tall houses seemed to act as echo chambers, throwing up disturbances from several streets away. A careless tourist might be mugged for walking down the wrong alleyway, prostitutes would fight with their pimps or their customers, and occasionally police sirens would wail when an incident went so far that they could no longer turn a blind eye. In addition, we would often be roused from our sleep by urgent banging at the front door. After hastily dressing and opening up, we would find a distressed prostitute, a desperate junkie, or someone bleeding from knife wounds.

Soon these broken nights were taking their toll, both physically and spiritually. The children were overwhelmed by the aggression they sensed everywhere, even among their school friends. Sally and I were being worn down, too, by the pressure of protecting Misha and Matthew and trying to ensure that we were meeting all their needs, while struggling to adapt to our own new roles in the city.

Sally went to a leaders' wives meeting where she shared her anxieties about our children. One of the ladies had a Scripture from Isaiah 43: "When you walk through the fire you shall not be burned; the flames will not set you ablaze. For I am the Lord your God." It meant a great deal to Sally as she shared this with me. We were grateful to the Lord that He would not allow our children to be permanently harmed by what they were being exposed to. We had known what we were going into and had our eyes open, but we also had God's peace.

God had brought us a long way since that first meeting with the beggar boy in India. As I stood on the bridge over the canal after our "funeral" procession, I had been reflecting back over the years - our time with the world travellers in Afghanistan, our move to The Ark and later Heidebeek and our latest move to the heart of the city.

The team workers were still talking to the crowds and the flaming torches gave off bright lights as they were held aloft. In the distance I could see The Cleft, which was now my family's home. Since Sally and I met the American beggar all those years ago, the Lord had led us in directions we had never dreamt of, but living here in the Red Light District was the greatest challenge of all. We never felt that we had made a mistake in moving to The Cleft because as a family we had all known the Lord's guidance, but sometimes I wondered if it was hurting my family too much. I felt particularly sorry for Sally and the children, who had been unhappy and struggling over the last few weeks. There were no regrets about doing God's will, but it was hard and we were under a lot of pressure.

I had relinquished responsibility for running the ministry at Heidebeek when we left and with the day-to-day running of The Cleft under the control of others, precisely where I fitted into the new work we were starting up in the city wasn't clear. In addition, we were helping to lead a large summer outreach, and hosting a steady stream of visitors to our cramped apartment - many of whom lovingly but unhelpfully gave voice to the doubts we were battling with inside.

By nature, I am an optimist but I lost my enthusiasm and felt discouraged. Both Sally and I were physically and emotionally drained: we needed to be practical and have some rest.

About eight months after we had moved back to Amsterdam, we were able to fly to the States for a short break. It came at just the right time. During that six week period we rested, prayed and studied and really enjoyed having time with our families and friends.

When we returned, it was with a new understanding and awareness of the spiritual battle in which we were engaged. We also felt God was increasing our burden to challenge other families to commit themselves to caring for the cities of our world. We discovered while in the States that many families suffer because they are *not* making sacrifices. We recognised that in a real way the difficulties of accommodation and environment we were facing helped us identify closely with the people we wanted to reach. We were learning lessons we could pass on to others who would do the same thing as us.

We came back with a fresh commitment that God had indeed called us to the city of Amsterdam, but the question still remained about our role in this needy city - how did God want to use us?

Twenty One

Walking in the Light

Amsterdam is notorious as the city of attics and hiding places. One such place attracts thousands of visitors each year. Tourists queue silently to squeeze up a steep staircase and through a secret doorway to shuffle into a small annexe where Anne Frank recorded her poignant diary during the war years. It is a moving experience to pass through the tiny rooms, tucked behind offices and a warehouse, where the young Jewish girl, her family and friends, lived in fear and discomfort for two years before being betrayed to the Nazis.

In many other attic rooms across the city, tucked away from prying eyes, are secret "goings-on" today that mock the courageous spirit of Anne Frank. There are dingy back rooms in bars and clubs where extreme sadistic and masochistic tastes are catered for. There are makeshift studios where the most chilling dramas are acted out for the hardcore porn market.

Recently, a government official announced that they now had proof of a child-porno ring that is kidnapping four and five year olds from Asia and South America and transporting them to Holland, Germany and Denmark, where the innocent children are forced to be in child-porno movies.

Amsterdam is the largest supplier of children's pornography to America, with over one billion dollars worth of materials shipped each year by a calloused and so-called tolerant Dutch postal system.

The sheer horror of the depths to which Amsterdam has sunk in pursuing its reputation as the sex capital of Europe was summed up for me by a visitor once who, having been shocked at the blatant scenes he had witnessed on the streets, wondered: "If all *this* is acceptable, then what on earth goes on behind closed doors?" It was a comment that echoed God's heart. One time when YWAM workers in the city were praying for the Red Light neighbourhood, trying to sense something of the way God felt about all that was going on, He whispered to one of the intercessors: "If only you had to witness some of the things I see, you would know how grieved I really am...."

Amsterdam's idea of sex is blatant, brutal and bestial. It is a multi-million dollar industry, supporting tens of thousands of prostitutes, and hundreds of sex shops, pornographic cinemas, live sex show clubs, and bars. While the lives of many of those who serve this monstrous industry are shocking, so are the attitudes of the others who quietly line their pockets from it. There are the people in positions of authority who happily exploit Amsterdam's reputation as a "risqué, liberal" centre for its money-spinning tourist potential. They aren't the only parasites who live off each other's flesh, there are the property owners - many of them elderly, "respectable" men and women, perhaps grandparents, who rent apartments for the girls to work in.

Around 180 guilders is the rent for an eight-hour shift in just one of the rooms. An average working man would earn this amount in two days. In some houses, there are three or four windows to a house, so the landlords have a lucrative business. Here we see that while everyone is a sinner, some are also sinned against. I believe that there is great wickedness in the hearts of those, removed from the glare of the streets, whose lust for money is satisfied through manipulating others, especially those desperate for money to care for children or to keep their drug habit going.

I am convinced that Amsterdam is a city under spiritual bondage. Years of submission to liberality and experimentation, through sexual immorality, have opened it up to demonic forces that control many lives: not just lust, but also greed. Man's sin and rebellion here have opened up doorways through which Satan has been able to enter many hearts, sinking his talons into the life of a whole city. We see this both in the lives of individuals and corporately.

In most major cities around the world, if it is not sex and pornography, it will be some other form of vice or commerce from which the greedy will benefit at the expense of the downtrodden. Our experience in Kabul had made us keenly aware of Satan's presence and work, and we quickly sensed his activity in the Red Light District. But in those early days on The Ark we felt that we were not prepared to tackle such a major stronghold of the enemy. Rather we advised our workers to avoid the area if at all possible, trusting that God would lead us into the district in His power, authority and protection and in His own good time.

Before any kind of outreach was planned, John Goodfellow and others led small teams into the city on prayer walks. They traced the route they would be following later, stopped at every point where a drama or gospel message was to be presented, and joined together in spiritual warfare through prayer. These times didn't only lay an important spiritual foundation, they also produced fruit of their own. During one early prayer walk John encountered two young girls who had recently arrived in the city for a wild time of drugs and men. After several hours' talking, both girls prayed for Jesus to come into their lives.

Such prayer preparation was also poured into The Cleft. For the first year or so after it opened, the small team based there essentially committed themselves to intercession as a full-time job. Up to four hours a day, five days a week, they toured the streets, praying for the people who lived and worked there and for a mighty move of God's Spirit. Tourists who passed them by would simply have seen pairs walking slowly along, apparently lost in deep, low conversation with one another. In fact, as they strolled and looked around, they were talking to their Heavenly Father, calling on His strong arms to be raised against the spiritual forces dominating the lives of so many people in the area.

We are certain that such slow and deliberate prayer was essential to all that has happened since. As in Afghanistan, we learnt at The Cleft that Satan could be both crude and subtle in his attempts to undermine us by trying to appeal to the potential for evil which I believe lies deep in every human heart. We had to be on our guard against his attacks. While vice in other major cities may have a discreet front, Amsterdam's facade is bold and blatant. So we looked for ways to avoid the temptations that were so often staring us in the face.

We learnt ways to walk through the area which would avoid the streets where the worst sex shops were. It is our policy always to go out in pairs, and never get into a situation where a male team member would be witnessing to one of the window girls on his own. We quickly got into the practice of praying for God to wash our minds and hearts clean every time we had walked through the streets, realising our desperate need for the Lord's protection from the spiritual pollution in the area.

But Satan could also be more devious. Shortly after moving into The Cleft I began to wonder, in my naïvete at such things, just how a huge illicit industry like the Red

Light District operated. What did people do in these places? How much did people charge? I mentioned this to Sally one night, and she warned me:

"I don't think that's a healthy curiosity, Floyd. You don't need to know these things to go on loving these people."

I could see that she was right, and I took her timely advice as a word from God. Many people who visit us in Amsterdam are curious too about the neighbourhood, but only rarely do we take them on tours of the Red Light area. We believe that God's Spirit will protect us if we are venturing out in His authority, but not if it is simply to gawk like many of the other tourists.

Many of the visual assaults on the senses have a greater effect on the men, and together we began to develop and exercise what we call "walking in the light", from the passage in First John, where the Bible declares that God is faithful and just to forgive us all our sins if we confess them to Him and to one another. We make a point of admitting moments of temptation and stress to our partners and close friends as soon as possible, seeking their prayer support in standing against the enemy. We try to open our lives to each other in humility and understanding and, as God so often does, He brings good out of potential evil. This mutual encouragement brings a special depth of fellowship, love and protection.

While the men learnt to seek God's protection on this level particularly, for many of the womenfolk involved in the Red Light ministry it has been a question of keeping a soft heart. Sally told me one day that in the face of such constant wickedness and evil, she found herself thinking that the people really deserved the problems they found themselves in. After all, what else could they expect? It was the consequence of their sin and rebellion against God.

"If I wasn't careful, I knew I was going to start getting

judgmental and stop loving the girls," she told me. "I was so overwhelmed by their sin that I stopped seeing them as people whom God loves. I've had to ask God to help me keep His tender heart towards them and He has been faithful in doing so."

Her experiences have been shared by many of the other wives and single girls, and some of the men, too. Sometimes our prayer meetings focus especially on this need to keep our hearts warm and soft in the light of such coldness and hardness. Such blatant sin is offensive and we found that as workers, unless we adopted an attitude of compassion and intercession, we would eventually become overwhelmed. We had to learn to see the city, and its inhabitants, through God's eyes and not develop a negative attitude to those we wanted to reach.

The sightseeing groups who stroll round with their guides as if they were viewing a stately home often stop to stare at the girls in the windows, to laugh and make rude comments or take photographs. On occasions, this has been too much for us, and we have stopped and confronted them.

"Excuse me, why are you doing that? This isn't a show. These girls are human beings. Why are you here?"

It has been surprising how swiftly embarrassment can cut a pathway through a previously crowded street. Of course, God is angered by the sinfulness of the girls and the Red Light area, but we also believe that He sees the hearts of all men and judges the "respectable" immorality of those who come to gawk.

One evening I was outraged to see a party of young secondary school children being taken on a guided tour of the neighbourhood. I went over to the teacher in charge and asked him just what he thought he was doing.

"These kids are probably under enough pressure over sex from their peers without you bringing them round here and exposing them to all this. Why are you doing this?"

The man was unrepentant, but curious when I told him about the work of Youth With A Mission in the neighbourhood.

"Do you know someone called Floyd McClung, then?" he asked.

"Yes," I answered guardedly. "Why?"

"Well, I've got this friend back home in the States who's a Christian. He tries to talk to me a lot about God and things, but I'm not really interested at all. When he knew I was coming over to Amsterdam, he told me to look up this guy called Floyd McClung. Not that I'm going to."

"That's really interesting, you know. You may not be interested in God, but He's interested in you enough to bring you to Amsterdam and let you know that He cares about you. I'm Floyd McClung."

The man looked surprised, excused himself and then went on his way, but there have been occasions when we have challenged tourists about what they are doing in the area and God's Spirit has opened them up to the good news.

We have also learnt what it means to wear properly the spiritual armour that God has given us, as Paul describes it in Ephesians 6. It isn't something that has to be done by "special people" or just those who live in a city like Amsterdam, but all of us must learn to live out our ordinary, everyday lives in the power of the Spirit. It means responding to people in the opposite spirit to that which we see around us - showing purity where there is immorality, peace instead of violence, forgiveness rather than bitterness, and generosity in place of greed and selfishness.

God often intervenes with powerful spiritual authority. On many occasions His Spirit has gifted us with words of insight or understanding, and supernatural ability, just when situations seemed impossible. Like the time we were out witnessing on the streets soon after moving into The Cleft. Our arrival in the neighbourhood had prompted a violent reaction. On the first few evenings we ventured out to stage open-air praise meetings and share the gospel, we were pelted with rotten fruit, and doused in hot water from some of the high windows. In such a neighbourhood, singing about the purity of a holy God aroused strong feelings of guilt and conviction.

Passing by one of the many sex theatres during one of these evenings, I was affronted by the particular vulgarity and coarseness with which the man whose job it is to stand on the doorstep and entice in passers-by described the attractions inside. Explicit language was commonplace, but he seemed to be worse than most so I paused to talk with him. The instant I mentioned Jesus, his eyes narrowed and he snapped at me: "Get lost, will you? I'm working!"

As I moved off, God touched my heart with a special awareness about this man's situation. My natural hurt at his rejection melted away as I sensed God showing me the man's inner heartbreak. The Spirit showed me that this man's wife, whom he loved dearly, had left him. He had two young daughters to bring up on his own. He cared for them deeply, and this wretched job was the only one he could find to bring in enough money. He was deeply ashamed of what he was doing, but felt cornered by circumstances beyond his control.

I turned and retraced the few steps back to where he was luring in the crowds. Standing in front of him, I tried to smile sympathetically. His eyes turned cold again, and I sensed another aggressive outburst.

"Look, I know you don't want to talk to me, but just let me say something before you shut me up," I implored quickly. "Is it true that you're married and your wife's left you?" I went on without waiting for him to reply. "And you've got two girls at home to look after, and this is the only job you could find?"

His anger turned to suspicion and then inquisitiveness. "How do you know, eh? Who told you?...."

"A friend of mine," I said deliberately vaguely, hoping to draw him into conversation. It worked. He forgot his hawking and we talked together about hurt and rejection and why a God of love would allow so much personal suffering into the world. God touched him in a special way that night. Soon afterwards he left the job, and managed to find regular work elsewhere. I don't know how his story ends, but I trust that there may be another chapter somewhere, some day, when God completes the rescue that He began that evening with His Spirit's empowering.

Spiritual warfare can be conducted simply by living out a faithful Christian life, day by day. Next to The Cleft is a large Satanists' temple, where services of worship to the Devil are regularly held. We believe that it was no accident that God found us a base in the Red Light District right next to this brooding, black-exteriored building which is symbolic of the Devil's doorstep to which God has called us. However, we do not feel that we should be engaged in direct spiritual conflict with the temple, rather we feel that simply by living godly, righteous, worshipping lives under the nose of the enemy we are winning a great, daily victory for Jesus.

This has been confirmed for us by the response our presence has provoked. Priests from the temple have stood outside The Cleft and our other buildings in the city and called down curses on us. We have also heard from fearful former members of the order, two of whom made commitments to Christ through The Cleft's work, that prayers are said to Satan calling on him to burn our place down. We were reminded of a Scripture in Proverbs which says "The curse that is causeless does not alight," and realised that we were not to respond in fear to these curses but to place our single-minded faith in the Lord.

One young man who had been involved with the temple, and who was highly disturbed as a result, came round a few times and threatened people at The Cleft with a gun. On another occasion, over a period of months, we were plagued by obscene 'phone calls and dead-of-night visits by a young man who claimed that he needed help in order to escape the order. Eventually, after spending considerable time in prayer, we felt that God was showing us he was a plant, a deceiver - rather like some of those early visitors to the Olfat Hotel back in Afghanistan. We prayed that his disruptive, draining influence would be overcome and within a short while this man stopped contacting us.

Although we were now actively out on the streets in the Red Light District as well as other parts of the city, all this still didn't satisfy John Goodfellow's evangelistic zeal! John and I developed a strategy of visiting the small clubs and cafes that are found all over the city, to play pool. We added our coins next to those lined up on the side of the table to book the next frame, and then casually struck up conversation with those waiting their turn to play.

"Hi, where're you from?" John would ask as he rattled a striped ball into a far pocket and lined up the next shot - he had discovered early on that winners stayed on the table and got to meet lots of new faces, so he had practised to make himself a respectable player!

"Me? From Dusseldorf," the reply would come.

"What do you do? What brings you to the city? Business? Holiday?" John would continue, adding a little chalk to the cue tip for his next shot.

"Here on holiday. What about you, what do you do?"

Casually, leaning over as he made the next shot: "Oh, I'm living here."

From there the conversation often developed and John told his opponent how he had experienced a life-changing encounter with God in Amsterdam several years previously.

One particular night John had finished playing pool, and on an impulse ducked into a noisy disco bar before going home. He ordered his standard tonic with lemon, and glanced around the interior, praying as usual that God would show him if there was someone inside with whom He wanted John to make contact.

John sensed that the man over in the far corner was the person God wanted him to speak to. He hesitated, as the man seemed withdrawn and unwelcoming. John had a distinctly uneasy impression that rather than striking up a conversation in the usual way he should simply go over, sit down, and tell the man that God loved him and wanted to forgive him. John reasoned to himself that the music was so loud the man probably wouldn't be able to hear anyway.

"If this really is what You want me to do, Lord, then You are going to have to do something about all this noise," he whispered.

A few moments later the music stopped in mid-song. The disco equipment had broken down!

Now convinced, John stood up and went over to the man's table. He sat down, smiled and introduced himself. He told the man that he was a Christian working in Amsterdam, and that God wanted the man to know that He loved him, and that He wanted to forgive him.

The man seemed genuinely astonished by John's comments.

"Do you know who I am?" the man asked.

When John said he did not, the man went on to explain that he was the high priest of the Satanist temple adjoining The Cleft! God was taking His salvation right to the Devil's doorstep.

Twenty Two

A Child Shall Lead Them

For the first year of its existence, work at The Cleft concentrated on laying spiritual foundations for a long term ministry. Our coffee bar was open to visitors, but the team's main job was spiritual preparation for the future. Prayer walks through all the streets and alleyways were followed by open air praise sessions around the street corners and on the bridges. Even this comparatively modest presentation of the gospel provoked an amazingly aggressive response, so we wondered what would happen when we actually started preaching!

In the early days of the ministry God gave us a clear indication of His personal love for the girls behind the windows. During a prayer time, Terry Goodfellow, John's wife, and Jan Baigent, a New Zealander, both found themselves with a mind's eye picture of a girl, a prostitute, As they compared the picture that had been given to them by the Lord, they were amazed at the similarity in detail. Expectantly, Terry and Jan began to walk the streets looking for the girl God had shown them. They toured nearly all the windows and alleyways before locating her in a little room at the back of the Red Light District. They tapped on the window and asked whether they could talk to her - and were brusquely ignored.

Heartbroken, the girls came back to The Cleft to share their disappointment. God had specially laid that particular girl on their hearts because of His individual love for her, yet she would not respond. In spite of the adverse reaction, Terry and Jan continued to pray for her regularly. This rejection was a sobering forewarning of all the struggles and rejections we would experience in the days to come.

On the other hand, our doubts about the rightness of taking our young children into the Red Light District were soon dispelled when we began to make our first tentative steps towards getting to know our neighbours.

While the adults found it hard-going, our children provided a way into the situation. Children and animals can melt even the hardest of hearts, and we were surprised and delighted to see how God used Misha, Matthew, the youngsters of other YWAM families and our dog, Pooh, to open doors and lives. They were not simply there because we had been called and they had no choice but to come along. Rather, God had a very important role for them to play in the establishing of our Red Light work.

It was not something we consciously considered as we started to go out for our family walks in the neighbourhood, but we soon recognised that having the children and Pooh changed people's perception of us. It was plain for all to see that we were not customers or tourists. We were just a family, out for a stroll, unlike other families living in the area who scurried their little ones past the windows with heads averted. We made a point of smiling and waving at the girls in the windows as we passed by, calling out a cheery "Hello". We hoped that these nodding acquaintances would lead us into a position where we could develop more meaningful contacts. It wasn't to be an easy transition.

With none of the barriers and prejudices of adults, the children were delightfully natural and unpretentious in their relationships. Soon Misha and Matthew and some of the other children were regularly stopping to talk with the girls whose windows they passed on their way to and from school.

In the summer, some of the girls sat or stood outside their rooms so it was easy for the children to speak to them. In the colder weather, they stayed the other side of their windows but because the children had been friendly to them, they would come to the door to chat. Sometimes the children just tapped on the windows and went in. They got to know the girls' first names and told them what they had been doing in class, often giving them drawings completed at school.

Misha took a particular liking to one girl who was rather more withdrawn than the others. She would regularly present her with paintings and sketches. Over the course of a few months, there was a real softening of attitudes, and a genuine friendship was struck. She began to visit The Cleft for coffee.

"Why are you so friendly?" she would ask us. "Why do you let your children talk with us - even encourage them to? Everyone else despises us and ignores us. What is it about you people?"

Gradually, other members of The Cleft team were able to share the answers to those questions - and the once hard-hearted prostitute became the first of our contacts to give her life to Jesus. Only much later did we discover that this was the girl Terry and Jan had been praying for and had met many months previously! She had known that we were from the same group, but had kept quiet about that previous contact because she wanted to judge the reality of our claims. She had been touched and warmed enough to open up through the children's contact.

Another of the girls who resisted our advances of friendship was one of the needier prostitutes. These girls are often drug addicts, whose expensive habits mean that they cannot afford to rent one of the window rooms. Instead, they hire cheap and shabby hotel rooms in one of the seedy back streets, and ply their trade out on the street itself. This is dangerous for them, as they are out there in all kinds of weathers, and often late at night.

Sally, who now had more time because the children were at school, passed this particular girl regularly on one of the small bridges over the canal just down from The Cleft, but her smiles and greetings were always met with a stony expression or a turned head. Sally felt especially burdened to pray for Cristal, and for a breakthrough in our contacts with her. This went hand-in-hand with the children's openness and delight in smiling at her and presenting her with the occasional gift of a drawing.

One day, as we passed by on a family walk, she didn't turn away. Instead, she smiled warmly, walked over to us and reached into her pocket to withdraw two candy bars for Misha and Matthew. It was a simple incident, but one that had a profound effect on us - affirming once more just why God was calling families to be the channels of His love in this needy part of the city. The children could open new doors for us.

In addition to our neighbourly contacts, our workers began a concerted campaign of visiting at night, when the neighbourhood sprang to life. Often we would be out late, until 2 and 3 am, dropping in to visit girls in the windows if we were invited. I was more than a little apprehensive the first time I joined such an expedition, even though we had prepared carefully in prayer and praise.

One girl who responded readily to our early visits was a pretty, petite Vietnamese who told us how her parents had been killed during the war. After seeing her brother die in a napalm attack she had been brought to a foster home in France, where she had been repeatedly sexually abused by the man of the house. She had finally run away and found herself in Amsterdam. Here she was soon drawn into prostitution, and had become the "special girl" of one of the most notorious criminals in the district, a man who was involved in the running of many sex establishments and a major drug ring.

Despite the horrors of the past, she was an open and friendly girl. She was always glad to see our staff workers when they dropped by, and began to show a real interest in what they had to tell her about God and His love for her. Unfortunately, her trusting personality may have been her undoing. She began to tell us about some of the serious criminal activity in the area, and of her fears and desires to make a break from it all.

We don't know whether she had a sudden change of heart, or someone took a dislike to her growing friendship with us, but she disappeared without trace overnight. All our efforts to find out where she had gone and why met with a wall of silence. Her disappearance was a reminder to us of the undercurrent of violence running throughout the neighbourhood.

Sexually transmitted diseases, drug addiction and beatings are some of the risks run by the girls working in the district. Sometimes the price they pay has been higher, as illustrated by a plain brick wall halfway along one of the busier streets which acts as a memorial. Behind it is an empty plot of land on which used to stand one of the district's most notorious sex and gambling clubs. One night a disgruntled employee burst in, doused the foyer with petrol and struck a match. Fifteen people died in the blaze.

If the children turned keys that unlocked the doors of some of the girls' hearts, then our cocker spaniel was responsible for a few others. Many of the girls kept dogs in their rooms - partly for protection and partly for company while they waited for customers. The antics and friendly nature of Pooh soon became a talking point. She was especially instrumental in paving the way for a relationship with dear Else.

Else shared a window-room with Sonje just next door

to us, and was initially the more reserved of the two. Despite all Sally's overtures, Else was determined not to be drawn into conversation. Then, one day, she commented about Pooh as we were walking past. Sally and I stopped to chat about dogs with her, and for a few moments we shared our mutual affection for animals. At last the ice had been broken, and Sally was able to make a point of stopping off briefly each time she left The Cleft to say hello, and pass the time of day.

Sally then decided to make subtle use of an old Dutch tradition to encourage Else to come out of her shell even more. In Holland, convention has it that on your birthday you play host to friends who drop by to celebrate with a drink and some tasty food. So she promptly asked Else if she could come round!

Else made excuses why she couldn't come, but on the big day she made an appearance. It was clear from her manner when she arrived at The Cleft that she felt really uncomfortable.

"It's kind of you to invite me, but I can really only stay for a few minutes," she said immediately.

Sally was on her own in the flat at the time. "That's OK, Else, I'm just so pleased that you were able to drop by. Come in, and we'll have a cup of coffee together."

Seated with a drink and a selection of home-made pastries which Sally had baked that morning - one of her specialities - Else began making polite conversation. As the minutes ticked by - five, ten, fifteen, then twenty - she thawed. She happily accepted another drink and a pastry and then, a little later, another. When she finally took her leave, to go and take her turn in the window, she had been with Sally for over two hours! As Sally told me when I got home that evening, they had been important minutes not only for Else but for us, in helping our understanding of the people with whom we were coming into contact.

Sally, who had celebrated her thirty-third birthday, was

staggered to learn that Else was not the same age, as she thought, but ten years younger! Her lifestyle had taken its heavy toll. During the course of the afternoon together, Else's sad story had spilled out. She had come to Amsterdam from the South of the country to find a good job, but failed. She then tried prostitution briefly, but had not succeeded, so in desperation she decided to return home, beg her parents' forgiveness, and try to make a new start.

However, the night before she was due to leave the city she went out for a last drink. In one of the bars, she was drawn into a conversation by a kind, good-looking man, who showed a great interest in and concern for her. They talked, wined and dined, and Else decided to stay in Amsterdam for a while. Over the next few weeks the handsome stranger courted and romanced her - and when the emotional seduction was complete, this sophisticated pimp turned her back into prostitution once more.

Sally was grieved and shocked by this sorry tale. It seemed particularly distressing because the one thing about Amsterdam's liberal and open attitude to the Red Light District was that girls did not need to have pimps working as their go-betweens. They could set up in a room on their own without having to link up with such men, who frequently abused them emotionally, physically and financially. Yet Else seemed content not only to work for her "man", and to hand over most of her considerable earnings to him, but to share him, too. For when she was working, at night, he was with another girl.

"I don't understand, Else. Why have a pimp? Why would you pay someone for friendship like this?" Sally asked.

There was a sharp intake of breath, followed by silence. Sally thought she had just burned all the bridges of understanding which had been constructed, when Else looked up with tears in her eyes.

"Well, Sally, everyone needs someone to laugh and cry with, someone to hug when you get home. Even prostitutes."

My heart was moved as Sally related the story to me. She added that after Else had gone, God showed her that she should not feel overwhelmed at trying to help someone in Else's position, but concentrate on being an honest friend to her.

That is what Else became over the next few months, coming round for coffee several times. Then one evening she invited us over to her apartment to eat. Her flat was just round the corner from us. Like financiers and lawyers, some people in the sex industry move further out when they can afford to, commuting back daily to their workplace, but Else preferred to live in the neighbourhood. She was proud of the financial rewards she enjoyed from her work, so that she was able to enjoy all the creature comforts and luxuries she wanted.

She showed us round the tastefully-decorated flat, and then led us into what at first I thought was another bedroom. It turned out to be an enormous walk-in wardrobe. It was filled with scores of pairs of shoes and new outfits in all the latest fashions. She delighted in showing us all her beautiful clothes, but inwardly we were heartbroken. Poor Else, taking off her clothes for strangers in one part of the city, so that she could wear nice ones when she met people in another!

Else was adamant that she knew what she was doing.She enjoyed expensive clothes and a comfortable home, and that was where her money would go. She maintained she would never get into drugs and drink like some of the other girls, because that was an awful waste. She appreciated the good things in life, and as far as she was concerned it was worth the hurt of working the windows to gain material possessions.

Naturally, during our time together the conversation

came round to the opposing views towards life, love and material goods which we held, but we never "preached" at her. We talked about Jesus and the way He shaped our lives, as we enjoyed each other's company talking about pets or current affairs and laughing together. We became good friends and Else was continually in our prayers, but we sensed the great spiritual battle which was going on beneath our relationship. One day it broke out into the open.

After meeting with Sally for coffee, Else told her quietly: "You know, I don't think our friendship can go on the way it is. We're totally different, and if we are to remain friends then I'm going to have to make changes that I'm not prepared to face. So I think that I should stop seeing you and Floyd, because it's too much pressure for me. I'm sorry."

Sally was saddened and tried to persuade Else to avoid retreating from such a good friendship. She asked her to think again about all that we had shared with her about God over the past months, but Else's mind was made up. She wanted her world of money and material things. From that day on, she turned cold towards us. For the next few weeks, Sally regularly stopped at the window to try to chat, and invited her round for coffee again. But Else always refused and avoided being drawn into conversation. Then, unexpectedly, Sally found a new face looking out of the tiny window - Else had gone.

The postscript to Else's story is perhaps even sadder. Sally was desperately upset that such a friendship had come to an end, and that Else had turned away. She continued to pray for her - wherever she was - over the next two years. Then one day Sally bumped into Else on the "Walking Street", a shopping district very close to The Cleft. Else seemed awkward - and looked pale and haggard. Her face bore the unmistakable traces of heavy drugs use.

"Else, you don't look too well, and you seem unhappy, too. Why don't you come back with me now and we can talk?" Sally pleaded. Her efforts were unsuccessful, and once more Else turned her back and walked away.

To us, she is still a friend, and we hope, and pray, that she knows that whenever she needs us she only has to call and we will be there to help. We trust that this prodigal does decide to return home before it's too late.

In many ways, the story of Else painfully illustrates the slow, demanding work of trying to shed God's love in the Red Light District. Thousands upon thousands of man-hours have been poured into this work by many people. But this square-mile of city hasn't changed dramatically. There have been rejections, high hopes crushed, setbacks, and at times a sense of real failure. In the world's eyes - and even from the perspective of some evangelical observers - our ministry has not proved a great "success"! One pastor refused to continue sending financial support to the single missionary sent out by his church, when she reported back home about her work with the prostitutes. "A waste of time" was the way he described her efforts.

Those of us who live and work here are more acutely aware of the difficulty of the work than anyone. To work patiently, prayerfully and painfully with each individual girl, taking months to win her friendship and trust, then gently and sensitively introducing her to Jesus, seeing her open to His love and healing like a flower coming into bloom - then only to have all that snatched away as she is lured back to her old ways - can be thoroughly demoralising. In our weaker moments we have questioned, as individuals and an organisation, whether we can really justify the cost - in material and human terms - of pouring out so much, and seeing so little return.

Then we are drawn to Jesus' story of the lost sheep - where the shepherd left the other ninety-nine secure to go and search determinedly for the one who had gone astray.

This is what we are doing in Amsterdam's Red Light District - looking for the few. This is the ministry to the one per cent. But it demands no less commitment than that given to the vast mission fields and great evangelistic campaigns of the world.

Just when we seem to have come to the end of everything we have to give, God breaks through! In our hearts we know that all the struggling and sacrifices are worth it, when one girl makes it.

Twenty Three

Giving Gifts to the Lord

Marika was one such girl. She was first contacted by Marietha Scheepers, a South African girl working with the Cleft team. It started when Marietha got involved with our children's school.

Since Misha and Matthew attended a Dutch school in the Red Light District, either we or one of the YWAM workers would always escort them there and back. Marietha frequently accompanied them and one day she was asked by the school if she would help with the children in the lunch care centre. There she noticed a little girl about four years old who looked lonely and unhappy. Marietha felt drawn to this child and tried to befriend her.

One Saturday morning as she was walking through the Red Light District, Marietha noticed the little girl walking hand in hand with a man. She went over to say hello and learned that he was not the child's father as she had assumed, but her mother's boyfriend. Learning that the mother, Marika, was ill and had a small baby, Marietha offered to help.

She went with Herma van Doorn, another girl on the team, to visit the family that afternoon. They lived on the Zeedijk, perhaps the most infamous street in the Netherlands. Running down onto the corner where one of our outreach centres is located it is the city's main drug trading centre, and in the stretch of a block and a half there are fifty bars, each with their own illicit sideline in sex, drugs or both.

Marietha and Herma found Marika in bed. There was little food in the home and a pile of laundry to be done. The girls spent some time with Marika and returned later with some food for the family.

Naturally and quietly, Marietha began to turn up regularly at this untidy home. She would make meals, clean up, and babysit when Marika needed to go out. Sometimes, when Marika was too ill to look after the children, she would take them home with her for the day and return them to their mother in the evening.

Marika admitted to Marietha and Herma that she was involved in prostitution. Her lifestyle was catching up with her and her body was in a state of collapse: she could not keep down food and was often unable to stand up. Marietha took Marika to the hospital for tests but the doctors could find nothing wrong.

Over the weeks, Marietha took food and clothing parcels to Marika from our "care closet". Marika appreciated these and began to respond to Marietha's love, faithfulness and concern. There were times when she asked curiously about the motivation for all the effort Marietha was putting into their growing friendship.

About three months or so after the first contact, there was an urgent hammering at the front door of The Cleft. One of our leaders, Jon Petersen, was surprised to open the door to Marika's man. He asked for Marietha because Marika was really sick, and needed help right away.

Marietha wasn't around, so Jon took Herma with him. They rushed round the darkened streets to Marika's flat. She lay in bed, pasty-faced and sweating. It was obvious that she was very seriously ill. Immediately Jon and Herma dropped to their knees by the side of the bed and began to pray, imploring God to spare Marika's life and make her well.

Her boyfriend hovered uncertainly and uncomfortably in the background whilst this prayer plea continued. Suddenly Jon and Herma became aware of a powerful sense of God's presence in the room, together with a certainty that evil spirits had their hooks into the lives of the people living there. They began to pray more earnestly for both Marika and her man. He suddenly burst out sobbing and Marika woke up.

As the colour flooded back into her face, she told them how she had experienced an incredible dream. She had been drowning, and shouting for help. Out of nowhere a hand had appeared, and pulled her from the water just as she was about to slip under for the last time. Jon and Herma told her quietly that it had been the hand of God. They shared with her again the great love that had prompted Him to bring them to her that night when she so badly needed help.

This dramatic intervention made a deep impression on Marika. She spent six weeks in hospital and the children went to live at The Cleft under the care of a tired Marietha. During that time many of our women went to visit Marika and share the Lord Jesus with her.

A few weeks later, just before Christmas, Marika called by to see us. She came with her young children on the day we held our annual Christmas celebration. It is a special time for the YWAM community in Amsterdam, when we get together to celebrate Christ's birthday. As is normal on a birthday, we give presents and tell the recipient how much we love and appreciate him. But this time it is Christ's birthday, so we "give gifts to the Lord!" After a time of prayer and praise, we take turns to bring our presents to Jesus. It may be a new song, or a newly written poem, a personal Scripture, a drawing, painting or performance of a new drama. One time a group got together and bought a table tennis table for the rest of the community - they figured God would delight in seeing the enjoyment their brothers and sisters got from it! All of us choose the most personal way we can of expressing our great love for Jesus, and our joy at being able to celebrate His birthday.

On this occasion, Marika watched in some surprise as our staff workers brought their gifts. They included a tearful couple who happily dedicated their new baby to God's service and a young Filipino man who stepped forward and laid his passport on the floor, telling the Lord he was willing to leave his home for ever if that was what God wanted. We had all been moved by these gestures, and they must have stirred Marika in a special way, too. For when there was a pause in the proceedings, she spoke out falteringly.

"I'd like to give something to God as well," she said, faintly embarrassed at her boldness in breaking the silence. "Only I can't really think of anything to give....except me. I want to give myself as a gift to the Lord."

So she did. Before a crowd of tearful and joyful YWAMers, she knelt down, her piled-up blonde hair and glittery, sequinned pants incongruous in such an attitude of prayer. Timidly, she asked Jesus to forgive all the bad things she had done, to come into her life and make it new. She closed her simple confession with words half addressed to God, half to us:

"Please don't kick me if I fall down...Please don't reject me if I can't do it...Help me..."

None of us could have known how prophetic those words would prove to be. For it turned out to be a rocky road to wholeness in Christ. The evil influences Jon and Herma had sensed in Marika's room the night they had gone to help turned out to be frighteningly real, and powerful. Despite hours of counselling and prayer, Marika's past life of sin and the claws which Satan had sunk into her held fast. Her boyfriend's strange behaviour the night of her healing became clearer when it was discovered that his mother was a spiritualist. She was now praying to the Devil that Marika would be sucked back into their world of drugs and vice.

It was a fierce spiritual battle, and our prayer warriors fought long and hard for Marika's release. It seemed to be to no avail when, after several wobbly weeks of indecisiveness, Marika finally let go of her wavering new faith and moved back in with her boyfriend. After a short time and much prayer, she was back at The Cleft, asking for forgiveness and help. This time we moved her in with Karen Lafferty, who is a fine musician and a mature Christian. She spent hours singing to bring peace to Marika's heart and prayed ceaselessly when she was troubled with nightmares.

The struggle wasn't over though. During her flight back to her boyfriend, Marika had become pregnant for the third time and this drew her back to him so she moved out to her old flat again. By now, Easter was approaching, and the whole YWAM community was bound up in the affair. Many hours were spent fasting and praying, interceding before God and asking Him to break through finally, decisively, in His power. It had been at the last date of celebration on our Christian calendar, Christmas, that Marika had made her first steps towards God - we wanted her to complete that walk to freedom before the next one, Easter. We knew that a human sense of obligation would not be enough to break the bonds that were holding her to her old way of life. Only God could sever the past.

On Good Friday, Marika and her boyfriend were watching the film *Jesus of Nazareth* on the TV in their home. When it came to the moving scene where Judas betrays Jesus, Marika choked. She began to sob: "That's me! I've betrayed Him!" She was grief-stricken. Weakened from not having looked after herself through her pregnancy, she collapsed in bed and fell into a restless sleep.

A few hours later, Jon found himself opening the outside door of our coffee bar. There in the darkness stood Marika, and her story tumbled out amid tears.

"I haven't come for you," she said, "I've come for God."

Despite her new determination, we sensed that Marika still wasn't going to make it if she stayed within reach of the environment where she had stumbled for so long. So she went to America to attend a YWAM Discipleship Training School and had her baby there. It was at this stage that God intervened again with one of those twists of His planning that make you look back and wonder how you could have been so blind to His purposes all that time.

Over the course of the previous year or so, we had developed close links with a small home church in a pretty little village called Hoogblokland, south of Amsterdam. Led by a lovely couple, Henk and Marian Rothuizen, this warm fellowship had been a great encouragement to us in our work in the inner city. They came in each week to help out voluntarily, and supported us practically and prayerfully in many ways. It was wonderful to know their backing and commitment to what we were doing. They joined our prayers for Marika as she yo-yoed in her commitment.

They invited her, the baby and the children to stay with them after her return from the States. At first, she went for weekends and a few days, and then finally she went to stay with them for an extended period. While she was there, through their love and support, Marika experienced God's healing and release in an emphatic way. We all knew that she had really been brought out of darkness into the full glow of His light. There were no shadows left in her life. The people at Hoogblokland poured their lives and their love into her, teaching her the ways of God, and showing her how to be a proper mother to her children.

Several months later, Marika returned to the Red Light District to work. She joined The Cleft team with a confidence and boldness, and was a powerful witness in the neighbourhood, particularly among the many girls and businessmen she still knew who could see the profound change in her life.

She then met up once more with Robert, a young man from the village fellowship which had nursed her through to wholeness, and they fell in love. Today, they have their joys and difficulties like any other married couple, as they establish a peaceful, loving Christian home for themselves and the three children, whom Robert officially adopted.

It was a long, tortuous, and at times seemingly impossible task to patiently bring God's love into Marika's life. There were times when we wondered if we would every see that final, definite breakthrough. For people like Marika, who come from such a background of evil, their initial commitment to Christ is in many ways the start of great problems. It can take several years of prayerful, loving support to see some of them through.

Twenty Four

I am an Amsterdammer

I gazed up at the tall, five storey building, once the Salvation Army headquarters, and tried to picture what it had been like when General William Booth visited Amsterdam. The majestic old building now stood derelict, facing the main square of the city, with its back to the Red Light District. The infamous Zeedijk was on one side, where most of the city's hard drugs are sold.

As the crow flies it is only a couple of hundred yards from The Cleft, but because of its location there is a different atmosphere here. One hundred and thirty thousand people a day drive or ride past the building. It stands as a quiet sentinel looking across at the Central Train Station on the opposite side of the Square.

"Some day you'll live there." I flinched as I heard the still small voice of the Lord. I recoiled at the idea. It was hard enough living in our tiny apartment in The Cleft but now God seemed to be saying our family would live in a building illegally occupied by junkies and prostitutes. "Where would it all end?" I thought to myself.

My mind drifted back to the time when Don Stephens had been looking for accommodation for his summer teams in 1973. He had been intending to use this same building, but his plans had been thwarted when it was taken over illegally by members of the Children of God who established their cult headquarters there. Don had then gone on to find The Ark.

Our interest in the building, built a century or so ago as a luxury hotel, was first raised while we were still at Heidebeek. Together with other Christian groups in the city, we met together and prayed that some day the place would once more be used to serve God. We took students from DTS courses at Heidebeek into Amsterdam for "Jericho Marches" round the building, claiming it for the Lord. We felt that a building with such a spiritual history, and in such a key position, should be used for God's purposes.

Over a period of time, we came to feel that God wanted it to be used in YWAM's work. Having walked through the interior on several occasions, it was not a prospect I faced with any relish! Years of illegal occupation, which had begun in 1977 when the Children of God cult moved out, had left the building in a disgusting state. The last occupants had been drug addicts and prostitutes, and their low regard for domesticity was evident in every room. In some places fires had been lit on the bare boards. There was human excrement and piles and piles of rubbish, including old clothes, rotten food, and in some corners used hypodermics and contraceptives.

It was heartbreaking to walk round and think that this indescribable mess had been caused by human beings. It was an indication of what a state their lives must have been in. Perhaps most distressing was the discovery of a thieves' hoard in one of the uppermost rooms. Tucked away behind some old panelling was a stache of purses, wallets and handbags - all snatched from unsuspecting tourists and discarded once the money and travellers' cheques inside had been used.

Our family were still enjoying the tranquillity of Heidebeek at this stage, and I hadn't shared with Sally my thoughts and feeling about going to live in Amsterdam.

"Lord, surely you don't expect me to take my family in

there, do you?" I asked in despair. "It's just too much. You know we've trusted you in some difficult places in the past, but this is beyond me."

After hours of wrestling with the thought of living in this building with my family, I said to the Lord, "I'm afraid I just don't have the faith for it."

Then I sensed Him respond: "OK, you don't have to do it if you don't want."

The initial relief that flooded through me was replaced by a cold realisation that I was saying "No" to God. I was disappointed in myself. Very few times in my Christian life had I not wanted to obey the Lord.

"I'm sorry, Lord. How can I think of such a thing?" I said. "Please forgive me. You know that I'm not strong enough to take this on, but I trust that if it's what You want us to do, then You will enable us to. I'll go and live there someday if that's what You want."

Even as I spoke, I felt peace and an excitement about moving into that giant rubbish hole of a building.

Not long afterwards, we had the opportunity to buy the building outright. A wealthy Dutch businessman who had previously shown an interest in our work offered to buy it for us - at a cost of around 600,000 guilders. It was a magnificent gesture, but as we prayed about it we knew that the timing was not right. We were not ready. Although we needed a headquarters for YWAM in the city, it would have stretched us too thinly in our leadership. If we accepted this offer now, we sensed, it would become a huge millstone around our necks. We needed to wait and trust God's timing. It was one of the most difficult decisions I had ever made. How could I explain it to the man who had offered to help us?

We turned down our rich friend's offer, and proceeded instead with our plans to renovate The Ark. We were faced with an ultimatum by the port authorities. Apparently The Ark should never have been given permission to moor where it was in the first place, and it could only stay on if extensive improvements were carried out. God's behind-the-scenes planning soon became apparent.

We went back to our businessman friend. "You know how you wanted to buy the former Salvation Army headquarters for us, but we didn't feel it was right? Well, if you still want to help us, The Ark needs a lot of money spending on it..."

The 100,000 guilders he gave us saved The Ark from being towed away and scrapped and allowed its important work to continue.

Later when we felt the time right to buy the ex-Salvation Army building, the price had almost doubled. Our faith and understanding of God's leading had increased in the meantime too and the building's particular significance became increasingly clear.

Some people questioned why God in His economy didn't let us buy the building when it was half the price. Later, we saw that if we had taken on the project three years previously, it would have crushed us - we weren't ready spiritually and we needed time to develop more leadership and to grow stronger. It confirmed what we had felt at the time. God showed us, as we struggled with the question in prayer, that He was more interested in people than money. It was another important lesson.

I also saw that God was testing me as a leader. Could I say "no" to a major gift of money? Some of our Dutch friends couldn't understand. Some even broke off their relationship with us, thinking we were getting too super-spiritual. Now I realise God allowed all this to happen to see if I would be more concerned with what He thought about us than what people thought. Would I fear the Lord or fear people?

When we finally did buy the building in the summer of 1980, we knew it was the right time. There was a great sense of peace, and God confirmed that the decision was right in many ways.

Our acquisition of "Samaritan's Inn", the name we gave to the building, also helped focus the rest of the country's attention on what was being done in the city. This was an important development, as often Amsterdam has not been regarded as part of Holland by the rest of the country, who have been offended and embarrassed by its liberality and immorality. Many Dutch friends were deeply ashamed that we, foreigners, should have to live there to tell the city about Jesus.

Once we had taken the building over, however, it soon became clear that we couldn't afford to carry out all the work we wanted to do on it. A massive clean-up operation had cleared out twenty-two tons of filth and rubbish, and made the place suitable for "indoor camping" for the one hundred or so volunteers who used it as a base for a summer outreach. But it was still a long way from what we wanted.

In its day as a Salvation Army centre, the building had been crowned with a huge sign, beaming out at night the declaration: "God calls you." It had been an impressive sight, standing out above the many other bright lights competing for attention in the area.

This heart cry of "God calling" wouldn't leave me. And when the financial picture started to get increasingly desperate, I was brought back to it once more as I prayed for God's guidance. We knew that He wanted us to have the building, that the timing was now right, but how did He want us to resolve the financial problems that were handicapping all we wanted to do? When I told folk that God wanted me to write a book urging people to pray for Amsterdam and then give it away free, they thought I was crazy! Even to me it hardly seemed the most obvious way of easing our debts, but I was certain it had to be done.

Over the next few weeks, I drafted out a slim booklet,

God Calls Amsterdam, which explained why He loved the city, and why people should pray for it. We then scraped together enough money to pay for a national advertising campaign to promote the book, and gave it away to enquirers. Thousands of people wrote in for copies. Then God began to put together all the pieces of His jigsaw so that we could see the complete picture.

Many of the folk who read the book were stirred and made a commitment to Amsterdam and the work we were establishing. They began to support us financially. Money started to pour in, just enough to meet the bills and allow us to carry on our renovation works. Equally important, they pledged not only to support us in cash, but also in prayer. At the same time God brought along people to help us just when we desperately needed them. Keith and Melody Green visited us, and later sent a sizeable donation. Our Dutch businessman friend also helped us with a generous contribution, having heard our story as he listened to an audio cassette of a message I had given in a local church. Dr. Bob Pierce, the founder of World Vision, came through Amsterdam at a time when I was giving up hope for the project, and he was a particular encouragement. Many Dutch friends also rallied round us. God knew that we needed such spiritual and material support and He provided it at just the right time.

Gradually, the transformation began to take place. Volunteer crews turned the former dining hall into a casual coffee bar with a bookshop alongside. Upstairs there were administrative offices and conference facilities and also guest suites and rooms for visitors. We believe that Samaritan's Inn now stands as a physical and spiritual symbol of all that God is doing in the city of Amsterdam.

Thanks to a gift from the Evangelical Broadcasting Network, one of the Dutch Christian groups who had been praying for the project, we were able to erect a new neon sign across the front of the building. A message now repeats the old Salvation Army statement: "God Roept U", while an English one alongside declares: "Jesus loves you".

The new sign makes the building stand out even more, and it soon became famous throughout Holland. Astronaut James Irwin, the Christian airman who was the eighth man to walk on the surface of the moon, donned a space suit and was hoisted high above the city on a crane to perform the official switching-on ceremony early in 1981. The lights blinked on for the first time in a sea of balloons and cheering faces. Amsterdam and the whole of Holland knew that God had His building back!

Although we were quite happily living at The Cleft throughout this period, the sense that one day we would make our home at Samaritan's Inn would not go away. I had mentioned it one day to Sally, and she had reacted with her usual unflappable calm. At that stage though, she hadn't seen the interior as I had! When she finally did, she was overwhelmed - but for an unexpected reason.

Over the years we have entertained all sorts of people in our homes - everyone from prostitutes and drug addicts to millionaires and politicians - but she has always taken the same time, trouble and concern over each and every visitor. By the time we came to move back into Amsterdam from Heidebeek, she had simply run out of creative ideas. Dilaram houses, The Ark and the Heidebeek property had drained her instinctive home-making ability.

While still at Heidebeek and aware that sometime in the future she would have to be creating a new home for us again, Sally prayed for God's insight and abilities to help her prepare. "After all, He is the great designer!" she reasoned. Over the next few days, in her personal devotions, she began to get pictures in her mind's eye of a series of different rooms. She could clearly tell the style, mood, colours, fabrics. At first she didn't understand what was happening. Then she realised that God was already answering prayers. She began to scribble down impressions and ideas as they came to her, and then tucked the notebook away for future reference.

When Sally finally entered the Salvation Army building one day, she paused at the doorway of a dirty little corner room tucked away on the top floor - and smiled. It was an odd-shaped little room, each wall a different size and shape, with awkward angles, and one, square little window tucked up high in a wall. It was not the kind of room you would ever come across again - and it was precisely one of those that had been shown to her in her prayers two years previously! That room is now Sally's personal study, her favourite room in our precious home that runs along the top of the building. But dreaming about living on the top floor of the Samaritan's Inn, and actually having the money to build a home from scratch, were two different things.

I talked this dilemma over with Loren Cunningham one day, and asked his advice.

"Well, Floyd," he counselled, "if you believe that it's really what the Lord wants - so that you can be close to all the different works you are involved with in the city but still live in the Red Light District - then ask Him to provide it in such a way that no-one can ever have any doubt whatsoever that it is God's will...."

It was, as usual, good advice. We often took visitors to see Samaritan's Inn while it was being transformed, and one day when we had been living at the Cleft for about a year, Sally was asked to show a visiting pastor round. He was George Gregg, from Faith Chapel in San Diego, California, and he was fascinated by the place and our plans for the ministry there. Then he asked Sally where we would be living. She told him how we hoped to have an apartment in the building one day.

"We'd like to help you," he told her. It was a thoughtful gesture, but we didn't think anything more of it until we heard from him after he had returned to the States. He had told his church of the YWAM ministry in Amsterdam, and they had agreed to pay the entire cost of building a family flat into the fifth floor of Samaritan's Inn for us! New walls, ceilings, floors, kitchen equipment - even a king-sized bed shipped over from America because we could not obtain one in Holland. They provided everything.

When we finally moved into the apartment, we all felt we had been let out of a cage! While living at The Cleft we were not aware that we had felt trapped, but now we had so much more space and freedom it was amazing. One thing we noticed was that we could now go a whole day without saying "Excuse me" and it was wonderful!

It is the biggest home we have ever lived in, almost 1400 square feet! In fact, you could squeeze just about the entire floorspace of our accommodation back at The Cleft into our living room. We love it. Sally has incorporated all her "prayer decoration" ideas into the interior design and decor, and the result is a warm, welcoming, relaxing home. When I return from one of my busy overseas trips or come in from an outreach on the streets of Amsterdam, I always appreciate sinking into the sofa and absorbing the peace.

Then I look around at all that He has provided, recall the time I told Him that I couldn't possibly live where He was suggesting, and wonder again at His patience and love.

Twenty Five

God Loves *People*

I don't normally like to lead people on tours of the Red Light District, but this time it was different. I felt I was to challenge a group of senior Christian leaders with the needs and opportunities the area presented. As we came to the end of the tour, we rounded a corner and headed back towards The Cleft. As we walked down the street, I realised we would pass two of the girls, Maria and Alice, whom Sally and I knew. It was a warm summer's afternoon and I could already see them leaning against the side of the building with virtually no clothes on. They were bound to say "Hello" and want to talk. They normally greeted me by name and I knew this could give a wrong impression to these men. Usually I did not stop to talk to the girls if I was alone, but what should I do in this situation? My mind raced ahead to what my respected friends would think and I considered a hasty detour up one of the side-streets. I could just imagine what these leaders would think of me, being on first name terms with prostitutes! Even as I thought of such diversionary tactics, I knew that it would not be honest to try and avoid the girls, so we walked straight on and sure enough, they smiled and greeted me warmly.

"Floyd! Hello! How're you doing?" Maria and Alice asked as they stepped over to talk.

"Hello, Maria, Hi Alice. How're you?...." and we talked

for a few moments. All the time I sensed my colleagues standing uncomfortably behind me. I wondered what they were thinking. Nothing more was said that day, but a few months later I was speaking at a conference when one of the men who had been in that party came up to me.

"Floyd, I'd like to have a word with you, please. Remember that day you took us through the Red Light District when we visited you in Amsterdam, and you stopped to talk to those two girls who had hardly anything on?"

"Er yes," I replied, wondering if I was about to be remonstrated with or cautioned.

"Well, I want to thank you," the man continued, his eyes filling with tears. "You see, up until that time, all I had seen were 'pimps' and 'prostitutes', but when you took time to speak with those girls and called them by name, I saw them as people for the first time."

That is what our ministry is about - people - and Amsterdam is full of so many different types of people, all with individual names and with individual needs. God looks down on the vast crowd in this vibrant fast moving city and sees not just a sea of blurred faces, but people He has lovingly formed. He cares about each one and longs for them to come to know Him personally. And this is not just true of Amsterdam, but of all the great cities of our world. Over the last century there has been a headlong rush into the cities by people on every continent looking for work, seeking a new beginning, or running away from problems. God sees not just a mass of humanity in these cities, but *people*. He hears the heart cry of each desperate person and grieves over their situation. He is calling the church, you and me, to respond to the needs of individuals, city people desperate for help and love.

By the year 2,000 the sixty largest cities in the world will have a population of over 650 million! It is estimated that over 85% of the people in the world will be living in great cities by the year 2010. Every month eight more cities reach the population mark of one million people, two cities reach the size of five million people and every forty-five days another city hits the ten million level!

Daniel Arap-Moi of Kenya has said, "The cities of Africa are a sociological timebomb ready to explode," and this can be said of most of the world's major cities. Unemployment, unfulfilled expectations, poverty, homelessness, injustice and oppression are just some of the reasons for this. I believe the cities of the world are crying out for people who care and for those who will bring the gospel in a loving and real way.

Many Christian leaders and organisations around the world are banding together to respond to the challenge of urban mission. YWAM works closely with the Lausanne Committee for World Evangelisation, Inter Varsity, Operation Mobilization, World Vision and many other groups and individuals to mobilize the church and respond to the urban challenge.

The city by its very nature points the way to the future. Cities are more than just places, they are processes. Ideas, movements and philosophies start in cities and then spread out in their influence via the media, arts and education to rural areas. He who captures the city captures the world, especially those cities which are trendsetters. There are some cities that seem to be like spiritual capitals, dominating whole cultures and continents with their taboo-breaking, norm-setting function - Paris, San Francisco, Amsterdam, London, Beirut, Peking, Soweto, Hong Kong, Moscow and many more play this role in modern society.

In the last few years, YWAM has taken up this challenge to reach city dwellers with the gospel. Evangelistic teams and centres caring for the poor and needy have been established in Tokyo, Seoul, Hong Kong, Manila, Djakarta, Singapore, Calcutta, New Delhi,

Mombasa, Nairobi, Johannesburg, Cairo, Madrid, Paris, Frankfurt, London, New York, New Orleans, El Paso, Los Angeles, Mexico City, Bogota, San Salvador, Santiago - and many, many more!

There is a mass movement of humanity towards cities, but ironically at the same time there is a mass movement out of the cities by evangelical Christians. In Jeremiah chapter 29 verse 7, the Lord spoke to the prophet about the situation at Babylon. He commanded the people of Israel, even while they were in captivity, to "Seek the welfare of the city, for in its welfare you will find your welfare." As Christians, we need to ask ourselves whose welfare we are seeking. Is it our own security and safety or do we put others first? We will not find safety and security by running from problems. If we don't go to the problems to solve them, then the problems will come to us! Suburbia is no guarantee of escape.

The most important lesson that Sally and I have learnt by living in Amsterdam is one which we believe applies to all Christians, that God wants to use families to reach others for Himself. To seek our own security and welfare, to be pre-occupied with our own comfort and pleasure, is no guarantee of happiness. In fact, the greatest happiness in life is found in serving others, wherever and however God calls us to do that.

Christian families can make an impact by just being in a city, showing their faith in everyday living and reaching out and caring for those around them. It always gives me a thrill to see God using the lives of ordinary people such as the McClung family to do this work. Here on the "Devil's Doorstep" we have so many friends, co-workers, brothers and sisters in the gospel, who live and work to spread the good news of Jesus' love. It is not just a job for special people, hyper-spiritual Christians, but normal people who know Jesus as their Saviour, and want to walk with Him in humility and faith. There are no verses in the

Bible that say "Well done, good and famous servant!" We are simply ordinary children of an extraordinary God who are learning, trusting, growing and serving together.

Never has there been such a period in church history when the church has grown so rapidly on every continent. God is shaking our world and His Spirit is moving among every nation as never before. We have to ask ourselves, "Do we want to be a part of it? Can we make a contribution towards this?"

When we are totally available to the Lord, the big question isn't where we live, or even which country we live in, but who we live for! The challenge isn't for all Christians to move into the inner city - the Lord may not want us there - but for us to ask ourselves, "What are our values and what are we living for?" Is it to please ourselves and have a good life materially or do we want to be part of the Lord's work, wherever that may take us?

On the coffee table in our apartment is a precious gift from Aunt Corrie Ten Boom. It is a framed piece of embroidery which she often used as a visual aid. One side is a tangle of knots and threads. It is only when it is turned over that the beautiful picture of a crown which has been created on the front can be appreciated.

"So often our lives are like that," she would say. "In all the problems and pressures, we only see the back part, the jumble and tangle of threads, but God fashions something special from another perspective."

I realise this has been the case with many of the things that have happened in our lives as a family.

Our time in Afghanistan was a valuable training period for us and without it, the wonderful things God has done in Amsterdam would never have happened. We certainly couldn't have envisaged all that has taken place when we set out on the Trail all those years ago.

We now have over twenty ministries in Amsterdam

spread out over the city and its suburbs, staffed by almost 250 volunteers and full-time workers. These have been established to cater for the different needs in the city, where we love people, give them our time and help them. John and Terry Goodfellow have also launched a ministry called "Go Teams" under the auspices of YWAM which takes out teams for short term evangelism to reach unreached people groups in Africa, Asia and Europe with the gospel.

Although the new Ark ministry is now on dry land, in a former children's home right in the centre of the city, the same type of work will go on there - loving people, helping them and watching them grow in their Christian faith. One of the original Ark boats has been remodelled and is still used as an outreach to punks and other Dutch youths. The other was so old it finally had to be salvaged.

We are planning to buy either a house or a hospital to use as a hospice for AIDS patients so that we can care for them with mercy and give them dignity when they are dying. We are doing research before actually starting this new ministry and are establishing a prayer foundation which we believe to be vital to this type of undertaking. In the meantime, some of our workers are visiting AIDS patients in hospitals.

We feel that AIDS will be a dominant social problem in the city of Amsterdam (and the world) in the next decade. In a recent Government report it was estimated that by the year 1999 there would be slightly more than 16 million people in Holland and just over 11 million of them would be carriers of the new AIDS virus if the disease continued to spread at its present rate. We ourselves estimate that one in three 17-20 year olds in Amsterdam is gay and sexually active which makes them potential AIDS victims.

Many city officials and some medical practitioners have had a hard time facing up to the AIDS problem and taking it seriously, because it would mean a radical change in the lifestyle of the entire city. Amsterdam is sustained by a huge tourist industry which is attracted to the free living lifestyle. The authorities promote the sex industry and advertise the Red Light District as one of Amsterdam's main attractions. It is my view, as a Christian, that to protect the city from AIDS they are going to have to face the consequences of the city's lifestyle and make radical changes. Obviously the authorities are loath to do this because it could undermine the whole economic system of the city. Therefore they are facing a tremendous dilemma. So far, we have not seen them taking the spiritual and moral steps necessary to protect the population.

We believe that in the future many will turn to the church for answers because a rootless, pleasure-seeking society, in time of trouble, needs answers and we want to point them to the answer - a personal relationship with Jesus Christ. Our attitude is that AIDS is a result of man's sin but that does not mean we should shun the sinners. We are all sinners and every sin deserves God's punishment. God has been merciful to us as Christians and we believe that we should extend that same mercy to others.

Recently Amsterdam policemen have contracted AIDS through pricking their fingers on the needles of drug addicts they were searching. Babies are likely to be infected with AIDS if their mothers are carriers and many others are affected by the disease through no fault of their own. We in YWAM are not adopting fear tactics or panicking or withdrawing, but we do feel we need to take sensible precautions, while at the same time maintaining loving relationships.

The YWAM community in Amsterdam hope and believe that one day the city's notoriety will be replaced by a reputation for godliness and righteousness the world over - a city more famous for its missionaries than its sinners. We believe that is the desire of God's heart too. Our ministry has grown to the point where Amsterdam is not only a place where we do evangelism, but also a place where teams are trained and sent out around the world. We want to challenge Christians to believe that God will claim their city for Himself as well!

We have started a Christian University in Amsterdam, something I would never have dreamed possible a few years ago. It is the European branch of YWAM's International University, started in Hawaii by Loren Cunningham in the mid 1970's, and ultimately we hope to see one on every continent. We have realised that in order to reach all parts of society we need to train urban missionaries who can work in the media, arts and entertainment, counselling and health care, government, education and science and technology. We have joined forces with 2,000 other YWAMers spread over thirty different nations in Europe to launch this university, and our goal is that eventually we will send five hundred to a thousand missionaries each year to work in major cities across the world. We want to train professional people to use the skills God has given them and to use their academic training to prepare them for a new kind of mission service to reach city dwellers with the gospel. I believe that in the next fifteen years 10,000 lay missionaries will go into the great cities of the world to take up professional roles.

We have discovered that Amsterdam is a great place to train people for service in God's kingdom. It is a wonderful "laboratory" for training in cross-cultural missions. With a population of one and a half million, the city is not too large to relate to and with one hundred and fourteen nationalities, it represents more than half the nations of the world.

Today Amsterdam sets the pace for sin - tomorrow we hope it will set the pace for salvation.

The Samaritan's Inn is the headquarters for the work in Amsterdam with its coffee bar and bookstore on the ground floor. Officially, I am the Director of our work in the city, and although I have overall responsibility for co-ordinating the work here, we have many capable leaders who share that responsibility. I have also been appointed Executive Director for the operational aspects for YWAM International and am involved therefore in the oversight of YWAM activities around the world.

Apart from looking after the McClung family, Sally is involved in lecturing, writing, hospitality, leadership in our work in the city and counselling within the ministry.

We still live on the "Devil's Doorstep". If it wasn't here in Amsterdam, then it would be somewhere else. Why? Because that is where the action is! I don't want to be sitting somewhere in suburbia, watching television, while God changes the world! I want to be on the frontline.

Sally and I dedicated our lives to reaching the world with the gospel. We only have one life and we want it to count to the maximum for God. I feel the way C.T. Studd, the great English sportsman, must have felt when he coined these words many years ago:

"Some want to live within the sound
Of church and chapel bell -
I want to run a rescue shop
Within a yard of hell."

Amen!

You are invited to join hands with Youth With A Mission-Amsterdam.

Amsterdam: The City...

...where *"anything goes"*—an internationally known urban center; often praised, often criticized. Her influences reach the far corners of the world: famous for her architecture, canals and history; infamous for her immorality, drug abuse and anarchy.

Amsterdam has grown into an influential, international center with 115 nationalities and 44 significant, ethnic groupings. A cosmopolitan city where the old meets the new—modern, glass skyscrapers on the edge of the city contrast with the canals and centuries-old buildings of the historic city-center. Known for her radical political influences, Amsterdam is also a center for artistic and philosophical innovation.

God has heard the cry of the city and is raising up a Christian army to overcome the strongholds of the enemy. Churches are being called to prayer, ministries are being raised up to *"proclaim release to the captives"* . . . on the streets, in the red light district, in coffee bars, discipleship communities, in homes, the classroom and among forgotten people groups.

This is our *"mission field,"* the place where the Lord has called us to establish *His Kingdom.*

Our Purpose is Clear . . .

We are committed to evangelizing Amsterdam and other great cities of the world by:
  ...proclaiming and demonstrating Jesus Christ and His Kingdom to this generation,

  ...living among the poor and needy, and

  ...mobilizing and equipping dedicated Christians for a lifestyle of evangelism and service in every sphere of urban society.

236

Our purpose is carried out through long-term and short-term out-reaches and intensive, practical training . . .

Long-term Outreaches: Since the birth of YWAM-Amsterdam in 1973, many long-term ministries have been established to reach out to the different ethnic and sub-cultural groups of the city all year round:

The Cleft is our "lighthouse" in the "red light district," reaching out to prostitutes, drug addicts, homosexuals and sex shop proprietors.

Samaritan's Inn Coffee Bar promotes friendship evangelism through a relaxed setting that offers a haven of "peace" for street people.

The Ark is a discipleship community dedicated to nurturing new converts and guiding others seeking for truth into a living, life-changing relationship with God.

Ethnic Ministries seek to bring the Gospel to those alienated by language and cultural barriers and establish fellowships within their people groups.

Neighborhood Evangelism Teams focus on ministry to spiritually needy neighbors through personal contact, Bible studies and lifestyle evangelism.

Church Contact teams offer leadership training programs for church leaders and seminars to equip church members in areas of witnessing and discipling.

The Inn Bookstore, located in a strategic downtown location, has special ministry to tourists and searching people as well as supplying Christian materials to the Body of Christ.

The Niteclub Team visits the discos and youth night clubs packed with "trendy" young people to help them find their true identity in Christ. They also have their own club, band and drama team. Punkers are coming to Jesus!

Child Evangelism seeks to share the truth of God's love clearly with the children of our city by means of Bible clubs and creative ministries.

International Christian Schools concentrate on evangelism through the education and training of children in the ways of God.

Short-term Outreaches: People enter the Kingdom of God one at a time. Through these short-term opportunities, you can be a channel for God to use to change a life. Not only will you see immediate fruit, but you will also receive inspiration and clarification on how God would like to further use you in fulfilling His plan for our world.

Summer of Service: During the summer you can be involved for 2 to 15 weeks in Amsterdam in ministries such as street theater, mime, music, preaching and personal friendship evangelism. Hundreds of volunteers join us each year to proclaim the Good News to this hurting city.

Global Outreach ("GO") Teams: traveling evangelism teams, well equipped with prayer and drama presentation, minister for three to five months each year across Europe, Asia and Africa, working together with local churches and pioneering new fellowships among unreached people groups.

Musicians For Missions: Christian musicians join together into ministry teams that proclaim the risen Savior through open-air and indoor concerts as well as leading church congregations into new depths in worship.

Training . . .

Training is a necessary part of all areas of ministry (evangelism, cross-cultural ministry, pastoral counseling, social work and administration). YWAM-Amsterdam offers a number of programs to help equip workers both practically and spiritually to better fulfill the call of God upon their lives. These are relatively short training periods which consist of class lectures and on-the-field experience.

Discipleship Training School is the foundation stone of YWAM's international ministry and is required before attending other schools or becoming a full-time staff member. The six-month course is designed to prepare you to be Christ's ambassador to the church and to the world.

In the first three months, you will receive teaching from outstanding Christian leaders and teachers from around the world in five basic areas: knowing God, understanding the Bible and how to use it, relationships with others, spiritual warfare and Christian service.

The second three-month phase is dedicated to putting into practice what was learned in the classroom. There are outreach opportunities in Amsterdam, Europe, Africa and Asia.

School of Evangelism: Amsterdam will be your classroom as you spend three months in specialized lectures on various aspects of

238

evangelism designed to equip you to be an effective and creative communicator of the Gospel. Teaching in the classroom on Biblical Foundations of Evangelism, Apologetics and Communication will prepare the way for practical training in street evangelism and learning to minister through the gifts and power of the Holy Spirit.

Following the School of Evangelism, there are optional outreaches you can take part in, both in Amsterdam and with YWAM world-wide. The Global Outreach ("GO") Teams are also sent out each spring at this time.

Amsterdam School of Missions is especially designed for those who have been called to cross into other cultures to share the Good News. Amsterdam School of Missions places an emphasis on reaching minority cultures in major cities. The two-year course combines language learning and missions theory with the practical aspects of commitment to one of the minority groups in Amsterdam.

Biblical Counseling School emphasizes the biblical foundations of counseling, healing of relationships, and the restoration of the whole man. The school is both for personal application of truth and preparation for ministry.

School of Biblical Studies: With an overview of the whole of Scripture as the goal, the emphasis in the School of Biblical Studies is on observation, seeing what the text actually says, and using an inductive approach of study. Skills are learned in exegesis and hermeneutics to enable the student to rightly handle the Word of God

School of Media Productions is a beginner's school of video productions, focusing on filming, lighting, portable systems, scripting and editing. "Hands on" training will be given with broadcast quality video clips, documentaries, and dramatic films being produced.

European Christian Institute: Seeking to have an in-depth impact on Europe, Youth With A Mission is starting a multi-campus European Christian Institute that will offer university quality education (to be called an "institute" until fully accredited as a university). Our vision is to produce graduates filled with zeal for the lost in an environment stressing academic excellence.

The purpose of this Institute will be to train Christians to serve in the "professions" with a view to bringing the teachings of Jesus Christ to bear on all aspects of life, including education, the media, government, science, technology, the family, and art and entertainment.

God Is Calling People to Amsterdam . . .

God has called us to reach the city of Amsterdam and through this city, the world. We need people with gifts, from pastoral to managerial—people called of God to undergird the evangelism, training and mercy ministries.

1. As a *volunteer*, you can come for up to three months and serve in an area of need or expertise.

2. You can be a *participant* in a short-term outreach in Amsterdam or on a mobile team.

3. As a *student* in our training schools, you will be exposed to world missions and learn first hand how God can use you to fulfill the "Great Commission."

4. You can become a *staff member* after successfully completing the Discipleship Training School. A minimum *two-year commitment* is required, but many have established themselves long term in their ministries here in Amsterdam.

5. You can become a "FRIEND OF AMSTERDAM"— those who commit themselves to regularly pray and give financially to the ministry and receive a monthly cassette tape with teaching and updated information on the ministries of YWAM-Amsterdam.

Youth With A Mission Statement of Faith . . .

Youth With A Mission is an international movement of Christians dedicated to presenting Jesus Christ personally to this generation, to mobilizing as many as possible to help in this task, and to training and equipping believers for their part in fulfilling the Great Commission. As citizens of God's Kingdom, we are called to love, worship and obey our Lord; to love and serve His Body, the Church; and to present the whole Gospel for the whole man throughout the whole world.

We of Youth With A Mission believe that the Bible is God's inspired and authoritative Word, revealing that Jesus Christ is God's Son; that man is created in God's image; that He created us to have eternal life through Jesus Christ; that although men have sinned and come short of God's glory, God has made salvation possible through the death on the cross of Jesus Christ; that repentance, faith, love and obedience are fitting responses to God's initiative of grace toward us; that God desires all men to be saved and come to the knowledge of the truth; and that the Holy Spirit's power is demonstrated in and through us for the accomplishing of Christ's last commandment, "Go ye into all the world and preach the Gospel to every creature" (Mark 16:15, KJV).

What Christian Leaders Say About Youth With A Mission . . .

Brother Andrew: "In this time of the collapse of organized religion, God is raising up an evangelistic, apostolic movement, one of the leaders of which is YWAM. I endorse their vision and cooperate with them in their recruiting and training program. We need not fail the Great Commission by not reaching a segment of the world's population. The opportunity is there."

Billy Graham: "One of the encouraging signs of the growing spiritual renewal in Europe is organizations like YWAM. They have hundreds of young people scattered across Europe . . . preaching, holding meetings, singing—witnessing any way they possibly can."

Arthur Blessitt (the man who carried the cross around the world; Los Angeles, California): "What a joy and blessing to minister often with young people from YWAM. Commitment, zeal, vision, and love always mark their lives as together we share Christ in our world today."

Pat Boone (Los Angeles, California): "Youth With A Mission is getting it done! When Jesus said, 'Go into all the world and make disciples of every creature,' it seemed impossible, even in the first century. But the disciples, under the direction and power of the Holy Spirit, reached the world they knew in their time. Never since has it happened again, until now—and today, under the guidance and power of the Holy Spirit, Youth With A Mission is crisscrossing the globe, interfacing with other committed Christian ministries, and getting it done!"

Ted W. Engstrom (president emeritus of World Vision; Monrovia, California): "I have long observed, with the deepest appreciation, the effective ministry of YWAM. I have witnessed first hand, in many places across the world, its program and noted the high quality of its dedicated young people."

Noel Gibson (teacher, evangelist; Sydney, Australia): "YWAM is a 20th century, worldwide, spiritual phenomena of evangelistic and mercy ministries fueled by the Spirit of God from a vision sparked in the hearts of a husband-wife team who dared to believe God and do His will. In the past 25 years, God has increasingly motivated, equipped, blessed and fulfilled countless thousands of people from all age groups and levels of intellectual, social, and church life who would otherwise have felt unqualified, unneeded, and unsuitable for effective Christian service."

Pastor Jack Hayford (The Church On The Way; Van Nuys, California): "YWAM is clearly a strategic and innovative development of the Holy Spirit's begetting for this challenging and difficult generation. The steadfast emphasis on commitment to Christ and His mission and the high calibre of leadership, both in leading the movement as well as being produced by it, invites the respect of people everywhere."

Rev. Paul Kauffman (president of Asian Outreach, Hong Kong): "I have followed with great interest the development of Youth With A Mission from its earliest beginning. We have often worked hand in hand for our Lord in Asia. I am delighted with the way God has used Youth With A Mission and wish them God's best as they begin their second quarter century of ministry."

J. Oswald Sanders (author and former head of the China Inland Mission; Auckland, New Zealand): "Two things impress me about Youth With A Mission as I have observed it. First, the breadth of vision of the leadership. They take the Lord's words, 'If you have faith as small as a mustard seed . . . nothing shall be impossible to you,' as being literally true. Second, the high level of zeal and commitment to the Lord and His worldwide program of young YWA-Mers, even though they may still not be very mature in other areas."

Louis Palau (evangelist, Palau Team Communications; Portland, Oregon): "The success of tomorrow's missionaries, evangelists and other Christian leaders depends to a large measure on the training our Christian youth receive today. I thank God for Youth With A Mission's ministry in providing *quality* training for thousands of young people worldwide."

Franklin Graham (Samaritan's Purse; Boone, North Carolina): "Through the ministry of Samaritan's Purse, I have had the privilege of traveling to over 45 different countries around the world. In many of these countries, I have had opportunities to meet representatives

242

of Youth With A Mission and have been most impressed with their dedication and willingness to go, literally, to the ends of the earth to preach the Gospel of Jesus Christ."

You are invited to become a
FRIEND OF AMSTERDAM.
Your partnership will help
meet the stated purpose of YWAM-Amsterdam
and touch the lives of the needy and hurting.

Write Today For
information on how you can receive
regular information from Amsterdam
as a FRIEND OF AMSTERDAM
or
how you can participate in
the outreaches and training programs
offered through YWAM-Amsterdam

Write To:
Youth With A Mission-Amsterdam
Prins Hendrikkade 50
1012 AC Amsterdam
The Netherlands
or
Youth With A Mission-Amsterdam
U.S. Support Office
1744 West Katella, Suite 22
Orange, CA 92667-9896
United States of America

Youth With A Mission - Statement of Purpose

Youth With A Mission is an international movement of Christians dedicated to presenting Jesus Christ personally to this generation, to mobilising as many as possible to help in this task, and to the training and equipping of believers for their part in fulfilling the Great Commission.

As citizens of God's Kingdom we are called to love, worship and obey our Lord, to love and serve His body, the Church, and to present the whole gospel for the whole man throughout the whole world.

We of Youth With A Mission believe that the Bible is God's inspired and authoritative Word, revealing that Jesus Christ is God's Son, that man is created in God's image, that He created us to have eternal life through Jesus Christ, that although all men have sinned and come short of God's glory God has made salvation possible through the death on the cross and resurrection of Jesus Christ, that repentance, faith, love and obedience are fitting responses to God's initiative of grace towards us, that God desires all men to be saved and come to the knowledge of the truth, and that the Holy Spirit's power is demonstrated in and through us for the accomplishing of Christ's last commandment, "Go ye into all the world and preach the Gospel to every creature."

Mark 16 v 15 (K.J.V.)

* * * *

As a mission we have also signed and affirm the Lausanne Covenant, which is a more detailed statement of belief and practice. It is available upon request.

Billy Graham says of Youth With A Mission:

> "One of the encouraging signs of the growing spiritual renewal in Europe is organisations like YWAM. They have hundreds of young people scattered across Europe... preaching, holding meetings, singing - witnessing any way they possibly can."

Dear Friend,

Thank you for reading this book. It may be that you, like some of the people in it, are searching for meaning and hope in your life. If you would like to know more about the Christian faith, please fill in the first box on the form below.

It may be, on the other hand, that by reading this book you have been encouraged to recognise that God can use *you* to reach others with the good news of His love.

We each have a ministry to perform, a place to be, that no-one else can fill. For my family and me it is the city of Amsterdam. For you it could be your home in a pleasant suburb, a modest town-house or a council flat. The important thing is not the location, but knowing you are where God wants you.

You will find the "Devil's Doorstep" almost everywhere. That is where we want to go with Youth With A Mission. We are an interdenominational movement committed to going to the tough places, in humility and faith.

If you would like to know more about YWAM, or how you can be involved, please fill out the appropriate boxes in the form below. We send out regular newsletters, a monthly audio cassette with a report on the work in Amsterdam and teaching by Floyd McClung, and a bi-monthly video magazine called *Global Perspectives*.

Fill in the coupon today and we will send you more information

☐ I would like to discover more about the Christian faith.

☐ I would like more information about your outreach programmes

☐ I would like more information about your work in ....(name city or country)

☐ I would like to receive the regular newsletter of YWAM Amsterdam.

☐ I would like details about the training programmes and European Christian University.

☐ I would like to make a contribution to your work. Enclosed is my gift of.....................

☐ I would like to receive the monthly audio tapes with reports about YWAM Amsterdam and teaching by Floyd McClung.

☐ I would like to get more information about your bi-monthly video report on YWAM worldwide.

Please send details to:

Name _____ (Please print)

Address _____

_____ Post/Zip code _____

Country _____

Post this form to: Information Services,
Youth With A Mission,
Prins Hendrikkade 50,
1012 AC Amsterdam,
The Netherlands